PUTTING
LIFE
ON CENTER

Brief meditations for
the prompting of daily personal devotion

Robert E. Luccock

ABINGDON PRESS
NEW YORK • NASHVILLE

To
Marietta Luccock Phillips

PREFACE

Airplanes and boats frequently travel on what is called the automatic pilot. Once the craft has been set on proper course the automatic pilot repeatedly corrects the drift or swerve caused by winds or currents. It is my hope that these devotions may serve a similar purpose for the person using them as aids to daily worship. Not that it will happen automatically; nothing in the life of the soul happens automatically—unless it be the drift away from God by those who practice no navigation of mind and heart. Rather that a person may be prompted by these exercises to correct whatever drifting he finds in his own life.

These pieces say little in themselves; they are designed more to *point toward* realities which the reader will find for himself. For the most part they hint rather than explain. They raise more questions than they answer, but they bear witness to a faith within which one may further search for truth and communion with God. It is hoped that from a quotation, an incident, or an analogy found in the few lines of each day's thought one's own imagination will be quickened to show him greater truth about his own life. The prayers prompted by the direction which thought has taken are offered as a *beginning* in prayer by which a person may come closer to God. The daily Bible readings are essential to the full exercise. In most cases the meditation depends upon the scripture for its understanding.

As an aid to the person who may wish to use the book as a resource for scripture themes and expository material the following plan is offered. Each of the thirteen cycles of readings recurs once in every quarter of the year and includes meditations on one central theme of Christian faith. Variations within each central theme are considered in the different weeks of the cycle.

Weeks 1, 14, 27, 40: Meditations on the greatness, wonder, and glory of God.

Weeks 2, 15, 28, 41: Meditations on the grace of God, his love for us in all ways, and especially through the Incarnation.

Weeks 3, 16, 29, 42: Meditations on Jesus Christ, his gifts and his work.

Weeks 4, 17, 30, 43: Meditations on self-examination, sin, repentance, and forgiveness.

Weeks 5, 18, 31, 44: Meditations on gratitude.

Weeks 6, 19, 32, 45: Meditations on personalities in the scriptures who journeyed into faith from unlikely beginnings, and more intensive studies of David, Mary the mother of Jesus, and Simon Peter.

Weeks 7, 8, 20, 21, 33, 34, 46, 47: Two cycles of meditations on the question from the prophet Micah, "What does the Lord require of thee?"

Weeks 9, 10, 22, 23, 35, 36, 48, 49: Two cycles of meditations on the life of the mind and soul. Taken all together these meditations form the heart of the book and stand as commentary on the words of Jesus, "Do this, and you will live."

Weeks 11, 12, 24, 25, 37, 38, 50, 51: Two cycles of meditations on the fruit of the Spirit based on Paul's summary in Gal. 5:22-23.

Weeks 13, 26, 39, 52: Meditations on trust.

These all appeared first in *The Christian Herald* from 1961 to 1963. They are gathered here with only slight revision through the kind permission of Kenneth Wilson, Managing Editor, and Daniel Poling, Editor of the *Herald*.

ROBERT E. LUCCOCK

CONTENTS

First Quarter

WEEK   PAGE

1. Doing Away with a Six-Foot God 19

2. No Strings Attached! 23

3. Living with Our Unsolved Problems 27

4. Your Beauty Has Made You Proud 31

5. Unsolicited Gifts 36

6. Journey into Faith 40

WEEK		PAGE
7. Count Me In		44
8. Can You Blush and Cry?		48
9. Skylight		53
10. Hard Facts or Soft Ideas?		57
11. A Man After My Own Heart		61
12. Please Pass the Salt		65
13. God and Our "Leftover Lives"		69

Second Quarter

14. Old Tales of Space and Time		74
15. He's Got the Whole World in His Hands		78
16. There's a Comfort of Not Running Away		82
17. Laying Aside the Purple		87

WEEK	PAGE
18. Giving Thanks in a Shipwreck!	91
19. King David—Loyal to the Royal in Himself	96
20. What Do You Put in First Place?	100
21. Putting Life on Center	104
22. Fidelity Outranks Inspiration	108
23. Keeping the Securities of the Faith	112
24. Clear of the Brooding Cloud	116
25. Footnotes to Faith	120
26. Staying Power	124

Third Quarter

27. Inside the Borders of the Possible	128
28. Which Way Is Heaven?	132
29. I Mean to Begin Again	136

WEEK	PAGE
30. Anonymous Evil	140
31. Lend Me a Dream	144
32. When Simon Becomes Peter	148
33. On the Street Where We Live	152
34. Exciting Adventures in High Fidelity	156
35. Walls or Bridges?	160
36. Never Disconnected	164
37. Mind Well the Minute Particulars	168
38. Head Over Heels	172
39. I Don't Understand All I Know	177

Fourth Quarter

40. Caution: God at Work	181
41. God's Not Killed	185

WEEK	PAGE
42. Fearless, Happy, and in Constant Trouble	189
43. Forget It!	193
44. Whose Love Is the Story of My Life	198
45. Mary, the Mother of Jesus	202
46. Your Religion Is Showing	206
47. I Will Not Be My Own Follower	210
48. Lift Anchor and Sail	214
49. The Saving Word Is "Yes"	218
50. A Candle Called Patience	222
51. Give Goodness a Beginning	226
52. The Sanctuary of the Ruins	230
53. The Moment of Truth	235

PUTTING LIFE
ON CENTER

The Lord is a great God.—Ps. 95:3

Doing Away with a Six-Foot God

Week 1——Day 1   **Read Ps. 95:1-6**

Coming from a session with his telescope, an astronomer remarked, "This does away with a six-foot God; you cannot shake hands with the Creator of what this reveals." He was right, as anyone would agree who has looked through a telescope or microscope. "The Lord is a great God." The psalmist who wrote that would not call God a "living doll" nor suppose he could be "buddy-buddy" with the Almighty, as so much irrelevant sentimentality suggests in our day. God is high and lifted up. He does know us by name, is closer to us than breathing, makes his dwelling with those who are of a contrite heart. But he is also the Lord of creation.

Whether by telescope or binoculars turned toward space, by magnifying glass or microscope focused on "the universe below our sight," or by our naked eyes lifted in wonder before the glories of creation, we do well to renew our awareness of how great our God is.

Thou who rulest the heavens dost also call us the sheep of thy hand. We bow before thy majesty. We answer to thy love. Through Jesus Christ our Lord. Amen.

Consider the two things which the psalmist says about God: "He heals the brokenhearted. . . . He determines the number of the stars." We praise God because he can and does gather our wounds into his love and give them some purpose of goodness and love. We praise him also because intuition and faith persuade us that the same Power which heals the brokenhearted also determines the stars.

We praise thee, Creator and Redeemer, for thy mercy and thy power, ever one God, world without end. Amen.

Who knows if the days of this year be marked for joy or sorrow, success or failure, blessing or tribulation? This we do know: God goes with us into the first days. He will be with us in the last days. God is Alpha and Omega, the beginning and the end and the ground of all that lies between. His love surrounds all this year, walks with us through deepest valleys, climbs with us up steepest slopes, crowns all the days with steadfast love, guards all the nights with peace and forgiveness. We shall not fear the unknown, nor fail to try great things.

O God, we take thy hand at the beginning. Hold us all the way to the end. In Christ our Lord. Amen.

The late President Fred Engelhardt of the University of New Hampshire was once heard to say, after taking a trip through the lake region and mountain ranges of his state, "I hope I'll never get used to it." The soul of the man who had grown so used to the glories of New Hampshire that he ceased to wonder at them would surely be dead.

Some have suggested that the deep sickness of the world comes from loss of the sense of wonder. We have grown "used to" beauty, to miracle, to the gospel itself, so that we fail to stand in awe and feel the glory of the Creator. We must never "get used to" God or to any of his works.

Our Father, help us to turn aside each day to see the wonderful works of thy creation and to behold them with grateful praise. Through Christ our Lord. Amen.

Week 1——Day 5   Read Ps. 139:13-16

The King James Version of 1611 translates the fourteenth verse, "I am fearfully and wonderfully made." The more recent translations say that God is fearful and wonderful. Both versions are true. In each the adoration is of God. In a normal life span your heart will beat 800,000,000 times, pumping enough blood to fill a string of tank cars from New York to Boston. By a single hair of your head you can be unmistakably identified. A tiny cubic half inch of brain cells contains all the memories of a lifetime. Your ear transfers air waves to fluid without loss. You are fearfully and wonderfully made. For all the "miracles" of life praise God the creator.

Glory be to thee, most wonderful God, for the wonder and glory of life thou hast given to us. In Jesus' name. Amen.

"When they heard this they were silenced." What an eloquent tribute that is! There are many kinds of silence—the silence that is afraid to speak, that doesn't know enough to speak, that doesn't care enough to speak. The silence of the apostles was none of these. Their silence was the sign of their wonder, their speechless awe and reverent respect for what had been done. They had nothing more to say and gave God the tribute of their silence. How wonderful when a person can be so perceptive as to see the mighty works of God in the least likely places and in consequence be overwhelmed enough to stop the clamor of his own speaking! Can we, even this day?

Speak, Lord, and let thy servant hear thee and be silent before thy greatness. In the spirit of Christ. Amen.

"False Christs . . . will show . . . wonders." And what wonders! Men have tried to make money their "savior," hailed the state as the new "messiah," looked to modern science as "redeemer" of the world's life. Wealth, nationalism, science, all have shown the most amazing wonders. We are easily led astray by spectacular signs of wonder-ful power.

God's Redeemer shall be called Wonderful Counselor, and to him alone shall we look for the interpretation of life's meaning, for deliverance by goodwill and suffering love. In him we find the greatest wonder of all—a love that never ends! The Greek word in Paul's promise does not mean that love always succeeds. Our loves sometimes dismally disappear, and who has not seen love go to some far country of forgiveness, only to receive rebuff? Love is never sure "to win." Rather, the love of God, revealed in Jesus Christ, will never disappear or diminish. When the love of Christ constrains us in moral failure, in suffering of soul, in the valley of the shadow, it is love unending and unfailing. This is the wonder of our God.

Forbid, O God, that we ever mistake size for salvation, but rather trust that there is no fading of thy love for us. Through Jesus Christ our Lord. Amen.

WEEK 2

God so loved the world.—John 3:16

No Strings Attached!

Week 2——Day 1   **Read Rom. 5:17-17**

Henry Ford is reported to have once said, "Never give anything without strings attached." He may not have meant it as it sounds; in some particular context such might be sage advice. At least you'll never be "taken" that way. But God attached no strings to the gift of his Son. He is ours to do with as we will. He never recalls his gift no matter what we do.

What have we done with the free gift of God's love?

May my love in Christ for all men be as thy love in Christ for me, without limit or condition. In Jesus' name. Amen.

General C. G. Bruce, gazing at the Himalayan giant Naga
Parbat, thus revealed its effect on him: "It gave one the feeling
that one wasn't there, and it gave one a feeling that if one
wasn't there it didn't matter." Oceans, skies, mountains, creation itself seem to overwhelm us into nothing. "What are we
that Creation should be mindful of us?" is an ancient question,
a common feeling. Then we hear the promise of the covenant,
as Jeremiah heard it. Then we stand before the Incarnation—
God with us—and we know we are not dwarfed into insignifi-
cance. We are of infinite concern to God. So persuaded we
become "able for all things," even the immensities of all creation.

*Humble us by the glory of thy creation, O God; then lift us
up by the wonder of thy love. Through Christ. Amen.*

J. B. Martin, in his early years of writing, found it necessary
to be gone from home for long periods of time doing research
for his articles. When his children were small they memorized
his face from a picture so they would recognize him when he
came home. Is that parable for how it is between ourselves and
God? Only we do the traveling here, into many far countries
of desire and idolatry, forgetting "how God looks." In Jesus
Christ we have a picture to memorize.

*O God, let us see thy glory in the face of Jesus Christ and
remember thee, and remembering, return. For thine own sake.
Amen.*

Edward Weinfeld, on becoming a federal judge, made his first act to find out what prison life was actually like. At one time or another, and through at least one meal, he has visited every federal prison in this country except two. "I'll get to those," he says. "I want to see every place I may be responsible for someone going." One surely cannot get the feel of it in one meal, or even one day. But most of us do far less than that to find out what life is like for others whose lives we determine. The judge was working on the right idea, and doing it with imagination. God went all the way. He came and stayed to see it through, suffering, death, and all.

Because thou didst empty thyself to become servant, I know that we walk no part of the way alone or without understanding. In Christ our Lord. Amen.

Antoine de St. Exupéry told in his book *Wind, Sand and Stars* of some Arabs visiting Switzerland who were captivated by a high waterfall. Their guide could not pull them away. "We want to wait until it stops," they pleaded. They could not conceive of water going on forever. We know that the steadfast love of God, like the Alpine waterfall endures forever. The unending flow of God's everlasting mercy is suggested by the refrain in the antiphonal psalm of today's scripture. Let it be our constant affirmation: "His steadfast love endures forever."

Thy steadfast love flows forever and is forever free. We are filled and we are grateful, our Father. In Jesus' name. Amen.

A writer has observed that two books were more frequently seen than any others in American homes of a day gone by— the Bible and the almanac. Often the Bible was an unopened fixture in the parlor, while the almanac, hanging from a nail in the kitchen, was consulted daily for weather, astronomical, agricultural, and historical data. We no longer have parlors in our homes but perhaps the comparative daily use of the two books has not changed in our time. Almanacs we still consult. But signs of the times that no almanac can reveal—what of these? Signs of our need for forgiveness, signs of our poverty without the unsearchable riches of Christ, signs of his appearing and his kingdom—what of them?

O God, in Christ thou dost speak the Word that interprets the world, the times, and eternity. We would see him, hear him, and heed him. Amen.

If God does not reward our goodness with prizes of earthly satisfaction, neither does he deal with us on strict reckoning after our sins. I may think I have not received what I deserve. But of this I am sure: I have been most mercifully dealt with according to my "badness." Neglected opportunities, moral immaturities, cruel indifference, hypocrisies, and waste—for all these my friends have been patient and God forgiving. God loves us with a love that sweeps away all this petty reckoning, and draws us to himself, no strings attached.

We thank thee, Father, for loving us when we do not deserve it and for cleansing away sin that we may be clean. In Christ we pray. Amen.

WEEK 3

But we see Jesus.—Heb. 2:9

Living with Our Unsolved Problems

Week 3——Day 1 **Read Heb. 2:8-9**

"We do not yet see everything . . . but we see Jesus." To so edit these verses and join them in one abbreviated text does not alter their meaning. The result is one of the great affirmations of faith, offering solid ground to stand on for those who are troubled. Canon V. A. Demant has put it another way: "Christian faith does not free me from perplexity: it does enable me to live with a lot of unsolved problems." There are many things we do not see—how some family problems will be solved; how our nation can solve its social and economic problems; how the peace can be secured. In the meantime we have hope and guidance for each day because God is still God, and we do see his power and his will in Christ.

Help us, our Father, to abide our unsolved problems knowing that thou canst make us able for all things. In Christ Jesus our Lord. Amen.

Week 3——Day 2 **Read II Cor. 5:6-9**

I do not understand all mystery. I do not know why goodness goes unrewarded, love is crucified, or righteousness defeated. I do not understand the mystery of pain or the destruction of fair spirits by hideous afflictions. Much of the Bible I cannot understand. But I do see Jesus. And I trust him for what

27

I cannot see, even as a child will trust a wise and loving older brother to lead him through some mysterious way.

I do not see all the way to the end of life's journey. I do not know where the journey will end for me nor what will happen to those I love. I do not know what lies ahead for the world. Sometimes I cannot see around the next turn. I walk by faith, not by sight. In Christ I see a guide for the next step, and in him I see the everlasting arms of a Father's love, a Savior's forgiveness to redeem life from destruction, and a home at the end of the road.

O God, I do not yet see all things saved. But in Christ I see the Savior. That is enough. Let my eyes never fail to see him and I can abide the mysteries I cannot see. In his name I pray. Amen.

Week 3——Day 3   Read John 4:1-15

We notice three things about this memorable conversation at Jacob's well. First, Jesus, the Messiah, appeared to the Samaritan woman in the simple act of asking for a drink. Second, he revealed himself to her quite unexpectedly; she had no thought that then and there she would encounter the Christ. Third, there was much in their meeting that was quite offensive to her. These same things we may expect to be true whenever we meet God's Spirit. He surprises us by his coming when we least expect him. He comes upon us in the most common of the day's events. He calls us into ways that are not easy to accept.

In the affairs of this day we would keep eyes, ears, and heart open that we may not miss thee, O God, when thou comest unto us in simplicity, in surprise, and in strangeness. In Jesus' name. Amen.

Week 3——Day 4   **Read Matt. 7:24-27**

A. D. Martin pointed to the scorn which Jesus had for every kind of laxity and for all feckless, make-it-do people:

The patch on an old garment, the misuse of old wineskins, the building of a house without proper foundations, the last hopefulness concerning a half-filled lamp, the loins ungirth. Jesus scorned them all. These are not the thoughts of a man who would use green lumber for seasoned, or daub with badly tempered mortar, or be too careless to use a plumb line.

Move us to shame for every laxity in our lives which the Master would scorn, O God, and let us measure everything we do against the plumb line of what is true. For his sake. Amen.

Week 3——Day 5   **Read Heb. 4:14-16**

Jim Harget told of the family who took a historical tour of the East Coast, stopping continually to read the markers along the roadside. Later the six-year-old son told what impressed him most about our country's past: "I think it was thoughtful of all those people to make history right along the main highways."

Christians have always felt the same way about Jesus. He has for us the saving power of sympathy and love because he traveled the same highways we walk. He was tempted

29

as we are, suffered as we do, died as we must. He made history that saves us on the street where we live.

Walk with us this day, O Christ, as we meet temptations and difficulties. Make the history of this day to reveal thy presence and thy power. In thy name. Amen.

Week 3——Day 6   Read Matt. 26:30-32

James Moffatt translated a portion of this passage, "You will all be disconcerted over me tonight." His word disconcerted provokes a vivid image of ourselves being disconcerted over what Jesus does, as indeed it should. Are you disconcerted over what Jesus does? If not, the chances are you have not understood it. Crucifixion is a highly disconcerting affair, upsetting to the smoothly arranged and organized patterns of life we easily fit into. Disconcerting not only in the ugly picture it gives of evil, but upsetting also because we see here where the love of God leads those who take it seriously. We will be disconcerted by what it means to take Jesus seriously in what he says about brotherhood and social justice. One measure of how truly any man understands Christ is how much Jesus disconcerts him.

Trouble us by thy spirit, O Christ, until we are uncomfortable wherever thy love is crucified. Amen.

Week 3——Day 7   Read Luke 7:1-23

Of the important things to be found in this passage none calls for more thought than the last two verses. Consider that the very reasons Jesus gave John for believing that the Christ has come are always the evidence by which the authentic powers and presence of Christ may be recognized. Those in the darkness of fearful prejudice see with the new light of faith; those who are crippled by fears and by riches walk trusting God; the impure are cleansed by beauty and by love; from those who would not or could not hear the cries of sorrow and need, these appeals now bring a response; those whose souls were dead have come alive.

William Dean Howells wrote to his sister in 1887, at a time when he was deep in Tolstoy, "I can never again see life in the way I saw it before I knew him." Change the reference and elevate it to an infinitely higher significance the truth holds: We will see life differently when we see Jesus!

We confess, O God, that we have looked for other saviors, but what we see done through Jesus Christ convinces us that in him is thy power, thy love, and thy life. Open our eyes that we may see him, and the world through his eyes. Amen.

WEEK 4

Search me . . . Try me . . . and lead me!—Ps. 139:23-24

Your Beauty Has Made You Proud

Week 4——Day 1   Read Ezek. 16:14-15

Here are two verses to ponder in every season of self-examination and repentance. James Moffatt translated the prophet in a provocative way: "Your beauty was perfect, through the splendour of my endowment—says the Lord the Eternal. But your beauty made you proud of heart, your brilliance depraved your wisdom." How close that comes! Beauty, personality, ability of any kind, for these we are grateful and in them we take satisfaction. It is no honor to the God who created us to undervalue any of his endowments. It is but a step, however, to become proud of heart over our endowments and to allow the stunning effect of brilliance to deprave our wisdom.

Lord, give us the grace of humility about our endowments. Turn pride of heart to consecration of gifts. For Christ's sake. Amen.

Week 4——Day 2   Read Acts 8:9

"There was a man named Simon, who [said] that he . . . was somebody great." Simon's descendants now are everywhere! It was said that King George III of England had a deeply rooted sense of his alliance with God. According to Thackeray he reasoned thus: "I wish nothing but good, therefore every man who does not agree with me is either a traitor or a scoundrel." King George made great mistakes because of this fault. So do we all when we do not confess our faults and flaws before God. Better far than an uncertain alliance with God is an unmistakable dependence upon him.

O Lord, save us from suffocation by the sense of our own rectitude. Instead of a feeling of alliance, grant us a conviction of our dependence upon thee. Through Jesus Christ. Amen.

A charming elderly lady said to the minister after hearing a sermon on Jesus' parable of the Pharisee and the publican, "Well, thank God I'm not like that Pharisee." The preacher, failing to note any twinkle of self-knowledge in the lady's eye, said only, "I hope not." We need regularly to stand off and take a good look at ourselves. The terrible part of Pharisaism is that you can have the disease and never know it. Without a saving sense of humor about ourselves we can never get over it. Ethel Barrymore put it in these words: "I suppose the greatest thing in the world is loving people and—and wanting to destroy the sin but not the sinner. And not to forget that when life knocks you to your knees, which it always does and always will—well, that's the best position in which to pray. . . . You grow up the day you have the first real laugh—at yourself."

O God, help us to laugh at ourselves and at our own pretensions. Enable us better to see ourselves as others see us and as we appear to thee. Then grant us the blessed discovery that thou art waiting to be gracious to every one of us who will turn to thy mercy. In Jesus' name. Amen.

People can stumble over "insignificant" trifles and so be offended at the Christian way. A small nail on a wide highway can puncture a tire and wreck a car. One mosquito can spoil the most magnificent view or the rarest conversation. In the same way some "unimportant" habit, some irritating mannerism, some offensive attitude can obstruct the Christian appeal that might reach others. Our own lives may deny the words we profess! A harsh temper, a cocksure attitude, a freedom seemingly without discipline—these may be stones of stumbling to those who will miss the Way on account of us.

O God, let us put no obstacles in anyone's way toward thee. We ask it for the sake of him who is the Way, even Jesus Christ our Lord. Amen.

Week 4——Day 5　　　　　　　**Read John 20:19; Rev. 3:20**

O Lord, with shame and sorrow
We open now the door;
Dear Saviour, enter, enter,
And leave us nevermore.

In our best moments we pray like that. But how many times we try to bar the gate to Christ! Into rooms where we keep our gold and silver we would rather Christ not enter. From rooms in which we dodge life's moral responsibilities we prefer Christ not to call us out. Let us examine our lives to see if there are rooms to which we have closed the door in fear, in shame, or in despair against Christ's coming.

O shame upon us to keep thee standing outside. Enter, Christ, with redeeming love and saving purpose. Amen.

Week 4——Day 6　　　　　　　**Read Matt. 7:1-5**

And, my friends, learn this . . . that just as surely as you think that any kind of fault or danger belongs wholly to another system than your own, and that you are not exposed to it, just so surely will you reproduce the fault or danger in some form in your own life. This surely is a good rule: whenever you see a fault in any other man, or any other church, look for it in yourself and in your own church.

These wise words of Phillips Brooks call us to self-examination, that where we must judge others we judge ourselves first and more severely.

O Christ, I will remember thy word; with what judgment I judge, I shall be judged. Have mercy upon me, for thy name's sake. Amen.

Week 4——Day 7   Read John 4:29

Some years ago, while painting the portrait of Winston Churchill, Graham Sutherland became convinced that "the impish Prime Minister was tampering with the work at night." Whether this be true, who has not tampered with his own portrait? We tidy up the face, cover the blemishes so we can like ourselves better. A true picture of ourselves is not easy to look at. But it would be better if we left the picture as God revealed us to ourselves in Christ. We would do well to put down the brush of tampering and let God show us all the things we really are.

In thy love I would face my true portrait. For Jesus' sake. Amen.

WEEK 5

*Remember all the way which the Lord
your God has led you.—Deut. 8:2*

Unsolicited Gifts

Week 5——Day 1   **Read Ps. 85:8-13**

During World War II the British Postal Regulations contained a technical description, "Unsolicited Gift." G. B. Stern once reflected thus on the term: "Parcel from America. . . . Repeat that curt phrase softly and slowly and kindliness will creep in. . . . Unsolicited gift. Like birth and the breath of life. . . . Like quiet and the sleep of death, solicitation cannot help to bring us these."

The words lift our thoughts far above the charity of wartime parcels. We depend for so much of life upon unsolicited gifts from God—the breath of life, the renewal of soul, the meaning of our existence.

Lord, we thank thee for all gifts which come every day unsolicited from thee. In Jesus' name. Amen.

Week 5——Day 2   **Read Deut. 32:7; Isa. 63:8-9**

In the conception and design of the new Coventry Cathedral in England is much suggestion for meditation. Consider the saving truth for life revealed in the materials chosen to build the cathedral. The pink-grey sandstone was taken from the same quarry that supplied the stone for the original cathedral in the fourteenth century. The baptismal font is a sculptured boulder brought from Bethlehem. In building this great church upon the ruins of the cathedral destroyed by the bombs of World War II men went to the same ancient source from whence came the first building, erected in faith six-hundred years ago. To the source of our faith at Bethlehem they went, for symbol of our faith that does not fade.

In whatever we build for the ages to come, let us remember the days of old, that thou, our fathers' God, may be our Savior, too. In Jesus' name. Amen.

Week 5——Day 3   Read Ps. 30:1-5

There is always a danger that in our prosperity we will forget the former urgencies of life; will not remember either how we were helped in our extremity, illness, moral failure, or accident; or will let it go out of mind how we felt when we were delivered. The psalmist who wrote these verses remembered how God helped him and gave thanks.

Most people have lived through some time of crisis when they were thrown back upon the mercy of God, stripped of all but his resources, and made to see how contingent life is upon the continuing mercies and providence of God. It is a necessary discipline to exercise the imagination day by day in recalling what we once realized in some urgent moment.

Help me, O God, to remember thee with gratitude and to respond to thy call with love. For Christ's sake. Amen.

This wonderful psalm of thanksgiving gives us four themes for unceasing gratitude. We allow verse sixteen to give wings to our thought this day:

> He reached from on high, he took me,
>   he drew me out of many waters.

Most of us will surely read that figure of speech as our own testimony. God draws us out of many waters—out the depths of failure by his unfading love for us, out the deep waters of sickness and trouble by his renewal of strength, out the seas of directionless drifting by the inspiration of his holy purpose, out the swamps of despair by his promise of life.

Thou hast drawn me out of many waters, O God. I am thankful for every rescue. In Christ's name. Amen.

Our gratitude arises today from the promptings of the nineteenth verse of this psalm of thanksgiving. "He brought me forth into a broad place." From the confining limitations of narrow prejudice God has brought us to the broad vistas of his love. From the inhibitions of our own faithless fears he has set us free for wider journeys of Christian adventure. From suffocation by the abundance of our possessions he has delivered us into his service. From bondage to time-bound and earthbound existence he has set us in the broad places of eternity and heaven.

Thou hast brought me forth into a broad place, O God. I am grateful for every deliverance. In Jesus' name. Amen.

"By my God I can leap over a wall." The psalmist perhaps thought in military terms; he gave thanks that God had enabled him to win victory over his enemies. But how many walls God has enabled us to leap! Walls of confinement by reason of affliction or accident—through imagination and a divine concern for life beyond ourselves we have leaped over walls of circumstance. Walls of self-pity—through praise and love of God we have vaulted out of the miseries of feeling sorry for ourselves. Walls of suspicion and mistrust—through a dependence upon the power of God that makes for goodness and reconciliation we have been empowered to trust.

Thou hast enabled me to leap over walls of imprisonment. I am grateful for thy lifting power. In Jesus' name. Amen.

He made my feet like hinds' feet,
and set me secure on the heights.

The hind is a mountain goat, surefooted on treacherous heights where nothing else can go except with great labor and difficulty. Many of us would thank God for this above all: He made us secure on the heights of danger. He gave us the ability to stand in slippery places where, in self-pity or a moral coward's fear, we might have given way to compromise and Christian betrayal. By God's grace we have now and again stood firmly where we ought to stand.

Thou hast secured me on the heights, O God. I am grateful for thy holding. In the name of Christ. Amen.

WEEK 6

I believe; help my unbelief.—Mark 9:24

Journey into Faith

Week 6——Day 1   **Read Exod. 3:1-12**

This week we consider seven people in the scriptures who made the journey into faith, starting from the most unlikely places. They should encourage us to begin the same journey even from where we are.

Moses was minding his own business, a refugee in Midian. God found him there, spoke to him through Pharaoh's injustice to the Israelites in Egypt, and persuaded him that he must become the servant of the righteous God of Israel. Any man's journey into new faith may begin at that same place—*with moral outrage!* Always in response to such moral demands the Christian journeyman may be sure of the Lord's promise: "I will be with you."

Thanks be to thee, Lord, for thy promise and thy presence. Through Jesus Christ our Lord. Amen.

Week 6——Day 2   **Read Ezek. 1:1, 4-6, 15-28; 2:1**

What a strange vision this prophet had! Of all its symbolism we cannot be sure, but concerning the central meaning there is no doubt. Ezekiel was an exile in Babylon. Among his people he found a great sadness, a hopeless fear: How can we sing the Lord's song in a strange land? It was not supposed that God could leave his familiar dwelling upon Mount Zion to follow the exiles. The prophet understood through his vision that God would go wherever his people went. We rejoice in the truth of such vision that we may begin our journey into faith in some personal exile where we now find ourselves—bereavement, lonely separation, enforced confinement.

Our understanding fails and our vision grows dim, but we trust thee to find us where we are, our Father. Through Christ our Lord. Amen.

Week 6——Day 3   Read Job 38:1-7, 31-33; 40:6-14; 42:1-5

In what an unlikely place God found Job—and Job found faith! His orderly world of thought was shattered. For all his "undeserved" sufferings there was no explanation. The tiresome justifications of his three friends were quite beside the point. Job could not take the measure of God with his small mind. Moreover, he told God so. Then God opened his eyes to the greatness and mystery of creation. And so even out of the ruins of disaster Job came to a profound personal faith.

With Job may we begin the same journey into new trust from the ruins of an older broken faith. Through Christ our Lord. Amen.

Week 6——Day 4   Read John 3:1-15; 19:38-39

Like all the Pharisees, Nicodemus had a faith securely buttoned down by legalities and traditions. Something in Jesus broke through all those walls, however, to trouble Nicodemus with intimations of a larger faith. He came to Jesus by night to learn from this teacher what his faith was. Something began in that conversation that changed the man's life. The only other time we see him is bringing spices for the burial of Jesus' body. Evidently Nicodemus turned in faith to the God of whom the Nazarene had spoken. Many Christians have begun their journey into faith in the same troubled perplexity of mind that cannot reconcile the old with the new.

By thy grace may we have the courage to seek the faith of Christ, even leaving behind older convictions that no longer express him nor serve thee, O God. In Jesus' name and through his spirit. Amen.

Week 6——Day 5   Read Mark 16:9; John 20:11-18

Many people begin their journey into faith, not with some accepted orthodoxy of belief, nor with some attitude of proper piety, but in the wilderness and waste places of sin. It is largely legend that makes Mary a promiscuous woman. Yet we may accept from the verse in Mark's Gospel that she had been a woman driven by alien spirits of evil. Out of such evil possession she had come to a love of Jesus, and that love had led her into faith. Most of us must begin the journey where Mary did, for alien spirits possess us—spirits of greed, fear, lust, pride. But they are no match for God, when we allow him his way.

O Christ, come with thy divine disturbance of our sin, that beyond the turmoil of repentance we, with Mary, may see thee, Risen Lord. In thy name we pray. Amen.

Most people will easily understand Elijah—discouraged with what he saw in the world, pessimistic about the future, baffled at how God's will could be so frustrated. How often we wish we could crawl away to some safe hiding place, under a broom tree with Elijah, having done with it all. What's the use? What good will further struggle do? Elijah felt so. He reckoned without God, however. God gave him a great thing to do—to help prepare for the future. Elijah would never see this future, but it was God's future. So it was worth doing in the face of every adversity, discouragement, and limitation. Elijah was to anoint Hazael, Jehu, and Elisha. To do these things was to find his way upon a journey into fresh faith.

Show us what we may do now, O Lord, to prepare for the days which are beyond our years but within thy providence. In the spirit of Christ. Amen.

If you think you are an impossible distance from great faith that could make a profound difference, consider Paul. See where God found him! As a young man Paul bitterly resented the Christian faith. He unleashed his hostility in destructive violence. On the very day that the great change came to Paul he was on his way to Damascus breathing threats and murder. The God whom he later loved, and for whom he died, reached down through all the hostilities to touch and transform his spirit. God is not turned away even by defensive hostility. It may be that such resistance clears and opens the way for a firmer faith. Begin where you are.

May we wrestle with all doubt and difficulty until we gain thy blessing, our Father. Through Jesus Christ our Lord. Amen.

WEEK 7

What does the Lord require . . . to do justice.—Mic. 6:8

Count Me In

Week 7——Day 1   **Read Luke 14:16-24**

In C. P. Snow's novel *The Affair* a man reflects upon the temptation to keep quiet when he should speak out about injustice: "There were always good, sound, human, sensitive reasons for contracting out [saying or doing nothing]. There is great dignity in being a spectator: and if you do it for long enough, you are dead inside."

On the other hand, what are the good, compelling reasons for "getting involved"? One is our common humanity; when a brother is being hurt our humanity says, "Stay with him." Another is our loyalty to Christ; his needs are one and the same with the least of our brothers. In faithfulness to him we say, not "please have me excused," but, "count me in."

We ask not to be excused from the struggle, but to be made strong to take difficult sides, O thou whose will is ever for justice. For Christ's sake. Amen.

The parable which Isaiah tells here was spoken against Israel. They did not nourish the covenant and commandments of the Lord, and their alien ways and idolatrous worship brought forth no harvest of righteousness, mercy, and peace. So God took the blessings away; Israel would lose the promises, said Isaiah. This always happens when we neglect the disciplines of justice and true devotion. In Sophocles' tragedy, *Oedipus Rex* Creon says to the condemned and outcast king, "You are no longer in authority here, but when you were, you served your own destruction."

Against this ever present and fatal danger E. L. Allen suggested a strategy for help. "We need to erect now and again across our path the customs barrier of conscience; for it is only as we are willing to be stripped to the skin of our souls and have our most cherished prejudices and delusions taken from us that we can enter the country of a new life."

Stand guard with us, O God, at the customhouse of our souls. Forbid anything to enter that would be subversive of thy holy will for righteousness. In Jesus' name. Amen.

It is well for us to be reminded unceasingly of the moral perils of our strength. George Adam Smith once wrote of the mood of Israel at the time of Amos:

There were all the temptations of rapid wealth. The growth of comfort among the rulers meant the growth of thoughtlessness. The upper classes were lifted away from feeling the woes of the people. There was a well-fed and sanguine patriotism, but at the expense of indifference to social sin and want. Religious zeal and liberality increased, but were coupled with the proud's misunderstanding of God: an optimistic faith without moral insight or sympathy.

O Lord, save us from ourselves, that our strength may not be our undoing. Rather may ours be the patriotism of justice. For Christ's sake. Amen.

Week 7——Day 4   Read Isa. 6:9-10

Out of Robert Penn Warren's story *The Circus in the Attic* jumps this line which jerks one up short: "They would not have believed him or his truth, for people always believe what truth they have to believe to go on being the way they are." That hurts! It tells too much of our own heart grown fat, our ears heavy, our eyes shut. We want to go on being the way we are. With T. S. Eliot's chorus in *Murder in the Cathedral*, "We fear the injustice of men less than we fear the justice of God."

Open our eyes, our ears, our hearts, to the truth that would change us from the way we are to the way thou wouldst have us, our Father. And enable us to suffer the change. In Christ's name. Amen.

Week 7——Day 5   Read Luke 4:16-30

"They rose up and put him out of the city." How unbelievable that his hometown should reject Jesus! How blind they must have been! But doesn't that verse tell a tragic tale often repeated since the unbelievable day in Nazareth? When God's justice has demanded some sacrifice of prejudice or of privilege, have we never tried to put the Master out of the city? When his purity has condemned our unworthiness, have we never tried to put him out of the city so we need not be reminded? When he has called this the time for costly decision, have we not put him out of the city, preferring to wait until some other time?

With shame we confess, our Father, that we have not always received thy truth. Help us to welcome Christ as master of our common life. In his name we pray. Amen.

Week 7——Day 6   Read Luke 4:31-44

"They knew that he was the Christ." In the light of modern knowledge we might interpret these events differently. We no longer speak of demons in the same way that the Bible talks of them, but of the demonic power of evil this world does not need to be convinced. The truth of this story is that *evil recognizes the challenge of Christ!* Evil resists Christ. Evil in high places fights reform and justice; prejudice stands against the hard changes Christ demands. Selfish fears and anxieties do not yield place to unselfish trust. But Christ can conquer if we seriously give him leave.

Come, thou Holy One of God, cast out the evil that possesses our hearts and dwell in us thyself. For thy name's sake. Amen.

Week 7——Day 7   Read Rev. 21:1-2

"For the former things are passed away." A good many former things have passed away in our time. The danger is that we will not see that they are gone or that change is inevitable. In the

Yellowstone Park geyser areas one now reads frequent warnings to stay on the established walks. Due to the 1959 earthquake the crust has been weakened and might give way if stepped upon. How many former things have been weakened by startling moral, social, and economic earthquakes of this present time? Racial patterns, economic nationalism, social systems of privilege—these are all passing away. We need to be aware of the new earth God would bring through changes in hard, established crusts.

God, we would not fall to destruction by trusting the insufficient crusts of ways outworn by thy righteousness. In Christ's spirit. Amen.

WEEK 8

What does the Lord require . . . to love kindness.—Mic. 6:8

Can You Blush and Cry?

Week 8——Day 1   **Read Mark 1:40-41**

According to legend witches cannot blush or shed a tear. What a horrible state to come to—not to be able to show either great shame or strong emotion, unable to cry! The condition is not confined to witches—many of us are so afflicted. Legend also offers the hope of a cure. Fall in love. When a witch fell in love she supposedly discovered the meaning of pity and remorse. In other words, she could blush and cry; she was human.

Faith confirms what legend imagines. To fall in Christ-like love for the family of men causes one both to blush and cry. To deeply identify ourselves with people, as Jesus did, to feel with compassion all their feelings, is to save ourselves from a hardness that is death. It is to find our true existence as human beings.

Lord, move us with pity for some person who needs the touch of love and the grasp of acceptance. For Jesus' sake. Amen.

Week 8——Day 2   Read Ps. 103:19-22

Stephen Paget, referring to Pope's familiar lines, "Fools rush in where angels fear to tread," made this turn of thought:

I am sure that angels rush in where fools fear to tread. There are many fools who are afraid of treading anywhere. . . . For instance, when the people next door lost their only child, there was a fool who left his card, because he was afraid to go in: but there was an angel who rushed in, and broke down, and cried, so that the other two found their tears; and it was time they did, or one of them would have gone out of her mind.

There are times when the Lord requires us to be rushing angels!

Lord, let us never fear to go where we are needed for Christ's sake. Amen.

Jeremiah wrote those words out of anguish and compassion. Certainly one mark of genuine faith and commitment is the extent to which we weep and pray with anguished intercession for the sons and daughters of the whole family of man. Four out of five people in the world have never had and will never have what we take for granted as a good square meal. Four out of five have never seen a doctor and never will. More than half the children of the world will never go to school. Seven out of ten of the world's population does not have sufficient access to press, radio, or television facilities. These are some of the "wounds" of God's people for whom our hearts will be wounded.

From embarrassing abundance we lift hearts in intercession for those who are poor. Remember them in thy mercy and move us to help where we can. For Jesus' sake. Amen.

"You get under my skin" is a way of expressing annoyance. In another way it describes the saving secret of compassion and understanding. Atticus, a character in Harper Lee's novel *To Kill a Mockingbird,* reminds us not only of a trick, but of a holy obligation. "If you can learn a simple trick you'll get along a lot better with all kinds of folks. You never really understand a person until you climb into his skin and walk around in it." Such use of his imagination enabled Jesus to feel the needs of people. He took their infirmities as his own. It may be that the Lord requires me to climb this day into the skin of another person and as far as I am able to take his infirmities as my own.

Release us, O God, from bondage to our own aches and pains that we may feel the pain of others who journey with us on the way. Through Jesus Christ our Lord. Amen.

Week 8——Day 5   Read Matt. 10:40-42

In Richard Hughes novel *The Fox in the Attic* Gilbert opposes his wife's suggestion that they take a homeless family to live in one of their cottages·

One's duty to mankind is a collective duty—not random little drop-in-a-bucket acts of kindness. Surely no one supposed he ought to rush off to Turkey personally to rescue a massacred Armenian or two? But he'd certainly make time to address the Armenian Atrocities Protest Meeting next month; and similarly his correct Liberal response to these strangers' plight was to campaign for improved National Insurance, more Houses for the Poor; not try to take these particular poor under his own personal wing. . . .

Bring our devotion down from love of mankind in general, our Father, to acts of kindness in particular. For Christ's sake. Amen.

Week 8——Day 6   Read Prov. 19:17; Matt. 25:34, 37-40

How well the man of wisdom put it in the ancient proverb: "He who is kind to the poor *lends to the Lord.*" Had you ever thought of your deeds of kindness as loans to God? Surely not with thought of repayment. Never! They are a kind of lending, however, and God does repay. Does not the king say in Jesus' parable, "Come, O blessed . . . inherit the kingdom prepared for you"? This is a return for what you did to the least of Christ's brothers. We are kind, but not in order to be repaid; the repayment will be one of the surprises at Judgment Day.

Whenever I see need this day, my Father, I would lend kindness and leave the loan with thee. For Jesus' sake. Amen.

Week 8——Day 7   Read Mic. 6:6-8

President James R. Killian, Jr., of M.I.T. declared a few years ago: "There has been avoidance, if not evasion, of the intellectual tax which must be paid if our intellectual budget is to be balanced." Has there been avoidance or evasion of the spiritual/moral tax by which the budget of our spirits must be balanced? "Taxes" are steep for one who would be faithful. Micah calculated the tax: *To do justice, and to love kindness, and to walk humbly with your God.* Have I paid my share that some may draw blessing and benefit from common life?

That which I owe let me pay without stint, for freely have I received and freely must I give. In Jesus Christ's name. Amen.

WEEK 9

To thee, O Lord, I lift up my soul.—Ps. 25:1

Skylight

Week 9——Day 1   **Read Ps. 27:5-9**

Henry David Thoreau found great ministries from a walk
in the woods: "Alone in the woods or fields . . . I come to
myself, I once more feel myself grandly related . . . I dispose
of the superfluous and see things as they are—grand and beautiful . . . I am not satisfied with ordinary windows. I must have
a true *skylight.*" Many have found Thoreau's skylight in nature. Others have found it in prayer; to lift up the soul unto
God and find him to be the very ground of our being is to
be "grandly related." By "skylight" we discover who we are—
the sons of God—and what life means—to be stewards and
servants of God's world.

*Our Father, let there be skylights for us, in nature, in our
meditations upon things grand and beautiful, in our solitude
with thee. In Christ's Spirit. Amen.*

Week 9——Day 2   **Read I Tim. 2:8; Ps. 32:10-11**

Toward the end of Galsworthy's *Maid in Waiting* one of the
characters is overjoyed because her brother is free from the
unjust charge that was about to ruin his career. The author
pictures her gazing at moonlit fields "trying hard not to believe
in God." This picture Galsworthy described with some amuse-
ment. But the further thought comes to Dinny: "It seemed

mean and petty to have more belief in God when things were
going well than when they were instinct with tragedy; just
as it seemed mean and petty to pray to God when you wanted
something badly, and not pray when you didn't."

*Our Father, let us lift holy hands of prayer in joy as in pain,
in loss as in gain. Through Christ our Lord. Amen.*

Week 9——Day 3   Read John 14:18-19, 26

A famous mystery story is built upon the idea of sympathetic
vibration. A detective had reason to believe that a stolen
violin might be hidden near the scene of the crime. Upon the
assumption that the thief had not loosened the strings of the
priceless stolen instrument, the detective walked through the
building vigorously bowing the strings of another violin, then
stopping the vibration while he listened. He was rewarded
when he heard quiet tones, sympathetic vibrations, coming from
the stolen violin locked in a hidden cabinet.

Is there not allegory here? The Master promised his Holy
Spirit to attend us in all our needs. Listening in quiet ex-
pectancy we may hear and feel the vibrations of his presence
to confirm us in strength equal to our needs.

*Let our spirits respond this day to the music of thy will,
thy mercy, and thy love, O God. Through Christ our Lord.
Amen.*

Week 9——Day 4   Read Mark 14:37-38

"Watch *and* pray"—these words spoken in Gethsemane sound
a warning to Christians at all times. We need to remember

both of them. Campbell Morgan, preaching once on this text, reminded his congregation: "Watching without prayer is curiosity; prayer without watching is superstition." Jesus commands us to do both. Some Christians are seemingly alert to problems, dangers, current events, even opportunities for God to work, but lacking any personal relationship with God that would give power, they remain reporters rather than participants. Others are so blinded by their piety they fail to recognize the signs of the times.

Our Father, if we are more curious than committed, send us to our knees. If our piety has made us dull, awaken our awareness. For Christ's sake. Amen.

Week 9——Day 5   Read Mark 6:30-32

General Griggs, a character in Lillian Hellman's play *Autumn Garden*, makes this wise observation that we forget to our immense peril: "At any given moment you're only the sum of your life up to then. There are no big moments you can reach unless you've a pile of smaller moments to stand on. . . . Most people like us haven't done anything to themselves; they've let it be done to them."

The daily small moments of re-creation in God's presence are the strength from which we will draw sustaining fortitude and an amplitude of faith for some "big" moment.

In this small moment we would touch again the hem of thy garment, O God. So may we prepare for the day when thy strength may be made perfect in our weakness. In Jesus' name. Amen.

A man traveled for five weeks through the Middle East and Europe. While he was gone from his home in Connecticut he kept one watch on Eastern Standard Time (home time!). "When I look at my watch I like to think of what my wife is doing back home." Is this not a parable speaking to every man of faith. Ought we not keep some reference to "God's time," our true "home time," where we can see it every day? What could this reference be? Daily prayer times, the regular reading of scripture, assembling together to worship, a cross, a quietness for meditation?

While we live in our times, help us to rule our lives also by thy time, our Father. In Jesus' name. Amen.

Henry Thoreau once wrote declining an invitation: "Such are my engagements to myself that I dare not promise." It is hard to know which is the greater danger, that a person have so many engagements with himself (be so preoccupied with himself) that he never becomes involved with others in the struggle to find identity, meaning, and purpose in life; or that he may be so ceaselessly involved that he never withdraws to know himself better or to be still and know God. We are endlessly reminded of the first danger; frequently we forget the second. Jesus brings it to mind. He did not always broadcast where he was. He needed his engagements with God and with himself.

Unless we have met thee and gathered ourselves in thee and to thee, what can we do for others? Meet us, our Father. For Christ's sake. Amen.

WEEK 10

Be transformed by the renewal of your mind.—Rom. 12:2

Hard Facts or Soft Ideas?

Week 10——Day 1 **Read Matt. 6:24; 18:1-4;**
 Gal. 6:7-9

Henry James recognized in himself the passive observer's tendency to transmute "a hard fact into a soft idea." It is a human tendency. Hard facts are unpleasant. It is much easier to sentimentalize childhood than accept the hard fact that we need to become like children in our humility, to accept the soft idea that we can serve both God and men rather than the hard fact that only one real loyalty is possible. It is a soft idea that we can sow just any moral seed and still reap a good harvest. The hard fact is otherwise.

Keep us, Lord, from softening the hard facts of the gospel to sentimental ideas of our own. For Christ's sake, Amen.

Week 10——Day 2 **Read Acts 2:40; Eph. 5:15-16**

A biographer has said of Bernard Shaw that he gave the impression, not of restlessness, but of urgency. "As though the spinning of the earth was something he ought to keep up with. And when seen on the London streets or on the Malvern Hills he always walks as though he had an appointment with himself and might be late for it." The appointments we keep with ourselves for thought, for discipline to the supreme priorities of life, for devotion to God, are among the most urgent appointments in any day's calendar.

Help us, O Lord, to walk wisely, making the most of some time each day for hard thinking, humble discipline, and earnest prayer. In the name of Christ. Amen.

Week 10——Day 3   Read Ps. 43:1-5

An editorial in the *New York Times* pointed out that many of the greatest scientific discoveries were made by what is known as "serendipity"—"the faculty of making happy and unexpected discoveries by accident." But as Pasteur recognized, "Chance favors the prepared mind." Great discoveries have on occasion come seemingly by chance. They are more likely, particularly discoveries of truth about life and values, to come to the *prepared* mind and heart. The mind is prepared by stretching for the great realities. It is prepared by continual renewal in grappling and probing for the truth. Let us be "prepared" for serendipity by the renewal of our minds.

Send out thy light and thy truth, O God, and let them lead us to thy dwelling. For Christ's sake. Amen.

Week 10——Day 4   Read Jer. 17:5-8

Christopher Morley once made this comparison:

We hear about the agricultural problem of soil erosion; hillsides denuded of fertile topsoil, or great regions of Middle Western richness scoured off by dust storms. Surely not less serious is the matter of mind erosion; the dust storms of daily excitement and of continual triviality can easily blow away the sensitive topsoil of the spirit. The result is a barren and shallow nervous credulity.

In a phrase from Jeremiah the consequences of such erosion are that we become "shrubs in the desert" bearing no fruit of discovery or faithfulness.

Our Father, may our trust in thee be nourishment for the life of mind and spirit. From daily excitement and continual triviality we would turn and fill our souls with thee. In Jesus' name. Amen.

Week 10——Day 5   Read Mark 12:28-30; I Pet. 1:13

A word that is little thought of in the Great Commandment is the word "mind." You shall love the Lord your God with all your *mind!* Loving God is strenuous mental business as well as moral exercise and spiritual devotion. "Gird up your *minds,*" admonished the writer of the epistle. Once when Chief Justice Taft administered the oath to six new senators, he made a slip of the tongue; they took the oath "without any mental obligation." No one can take the Christian oath without obligation to a lifetime of hard study and painful thought.

Lord, gird up our minds out of all laziness that we may love thee more fully. For Christ's sake. Amen.

Week 10——Day 6   Read Lam. 3:25-29

"Let him sit alone in silence," counseled the writer of Lamentations. Many centuries later Pascal put it that most of the disorders and evils in life were the result of man's inability to sit alone and think. Are men afraid to be alone with their own thoughts? Is this why music sounds out in almost every public place, why we keep radios and television sets constantly turned on? Can great thoughts ever come through screens of distraction? Can God's still small voice be heard above the din? Do you keep any islands of silence where you may think great thoughts without interruption, entertain troubled thoughts without confusion, seek after God's thoughts without distraction?

We would now be still and know that thou art God, all wise and all sufficient for our needs. In Jesus' name. Amen.

Week 10——Day 7   Read Phil. 4:8-9

These are the words of Van Wyck Brooks in *The Opinions of Oliver Allston:*

How delightful is the company of generous people, who overlook trifles and keep their minds instinctively fixed on whatever is good and positive in the world about them. People of small caliber are always carping . . . magnanimous people have no vanity, no jealousy . . . they feed on the true and solid wherever they find it.

That is a good way to live. From time to time a person needs to strike a trial balance: Is he more given to carping than to putting the bite of his mind into the true and solid?

We would be magnanimous, O God, finding the true and solid wherever we go. In Christ's spirit. Amen.

The fruit of the Spirit is love.—Gal. 5:22

A Man After My Own Heart

Week 11——Day 1   **Read Acts 13:13-25**

A man after my own heart. So we sometimes speak of someone who is a favorite. Literally it means one who follows after the way of my heart, who loves the things I love. David was a man after God's heart, who would do all God's will. This description Paul quoted from I Samuel. We might well drop the phrase deep into memory. What would it mean to be after God's heart? The prophet tells us it would mean to deal justly with all people, to be sure that whatever we do be done with mercy, to live always in humility before the greatness of God. These are impossible achievements—unless one lives *in the Spirit.* The fruit of yielding life to the sway of God's Spirit is love.

In all that I do this day may I be after thy heart, O God, humbly intent upon the justice and mercy of thy desiring. In the Spirit of Christ. Amen.

Week 11——Day 2   **Read Phil. 4:8-9**

Saint John-of-the-Cross put the truth of Paul's words in another way: "The soul lives by that which it loves and not by the body which it animates." History offers many instances of this truth. Gandhi really lived by the things he loved rather than by his frail little body. Helen Keller, Beethoven, Franklin Roosevelt—many come to mind whose souls drew their lives from their loves, not from afflicted bodies. Paul told us what things we ought to think upon and to love if we would have the peace of God. Whatever things we love determine what kind of soul will animate our bodies and our existence.

Search me, O God, and know my heart, and lead me by my love of whatever is true, lovely, and worthy of praise in the way everlasting. In Jesus' name. Amen.

Week 11——Day 3   **Read Hos. 3:1-3**

In Lorraine Hansberry's play *A Raisin in the Sun* the mother cries out, when the others condemn the ambitious boy who has squandered the family fortune, that you do not love people only when they do good. You need to love them most when they fail. This truth God revealed to Hosea—that he must love the one who has betrayed him the most. God's love for us gives the Spirit without which such love for others would be impossible.

Give us grace, O God, to love the unlovely even as God loves us when we are least lovable. In Christ's Spirit. Amen.

Week 11——Day 4   **Read Mark 6:40-44**

How Jesus multiplied the bread to feed a vast crowd I do not know, but I do not doubt what God can do with the little we give him, multiplying meager offerings—an obscure act of mercy, a quiet testimony of faith, a small loaf of some faithful performance—into considerable consequences. Have we not seen God break the loaf so that many have been satisfied and fragments gathered up long after?

In many a wilderness God has broken a loaf to us: Someone wrote a letter of encouragement; a family gave the common expression of love; someone forgave a wrong we had done. None realized what God would do with these loaves, but ever after we have gathered up fragments to fill the years. Who could reckon how many have been satisfied? The miracle of the breaking of the loaves to feed a multitude never ends.

Lord, I thank thee that I have been fed with the bread of life broken to me in the love of Christ. Give me faith to trust the offering of what I have to thee. Do thou divide it as may be best for all. In Christ's Spirit. Amen.

Week 11— Day 5   **Read Rom. 12:10**

A squib in a paper said that James Whistler and Oscar Wilde had been seen at Brighton talking, as usual, about themselves. Whistler sent Wilde the clipping with the comment, "I wish these reporters would be accurate; if you remember, Oscar, we were talking about me." Immediately Wilde telegraphed back, "It's true, Jimmie, we were talking about you, but I was thinking about myself." That comes close to home! How much greater understanding and compassion were we to heed Paul's counsel to the Romans, "in honor preferring one another (K.J.V.)."

When we listen, O God, let us truly hear our neighbor, and when we speak let it be in preference of him. In Jesus' name. Amen.

Jules Feiffer wrote a delightful parable in *Holiday* magazine which concludes thus: "Excalibur brought Rose back to his village, and they built a house with eight sides. One side was for frivolity, one side was for solemnity. And the six spare sides were for whatever new knowledge of themselves and of the world their future together might bring." These are superb rules for the building of every home—a side for frivolity, a side for solemnity, and plenty of sides to support new knowledge as we change and grow. How many sides does your home have?

O Lord, let there be in our homes the fruit of the Spirit: holy frivolity, joyous solemnity, and abundance of room to grow. In Jesus' name. Amen.

In one of the choruses from Aeschylus' tragedy *Orestes*, are the words: "It is the eternal rule that drops of blood spilt on the ground demand yet other blood." This should speak to Christian imagination, not in the sense of retribution—blood for blood—but in another sense. Because blood has been spilled for us by those who died on our behalf, by those who poured out their life's blood in suffering and sacrifice for our sakes—above all by Christ himself—we must spill our own blood for the sake of what has been given to us. To what great purposes are we committed, even to great suffering, in response to the great suffering offered for us?

Our Father, bring to our awareness the full measure of blood, sweat, toil, and tears poured out for us, and make us ready to return the same unto thee. For Christ's sake. Amen.

WEEK 12

The fruit of the Spirit is . . . joy.—Gal. 5:22

Please Pass the Salt

Week 12——Day 1   **Read Mark 9:42-50**

"Have salt in yourselves, and be at peace with one another."
This interesting verse Torrey translates, "Have salt in yourselves and pass it on to your fellows." Salt preserves life from
being spoiled. So, please pass the salt! Pass on the fruit of the
Spirit which has come to you by faith to others in the company
who make life's journey with you. Let the confidence of your
trust in God be known to those who are fearful. Give the
strength of your resolve to stand firm against evil to a person
who may waver. And please pass some of the joy of the Lord
to others who are having a hard time.

*Show us this day, O Lord, to whom we may pass the salt
of the good life in Christ. For his sake. Amen.*

Week 12——Day 2   **Read Luke 15:3-7**

Dean William Inge of St. Paul's, London, became known as
"the gloomy dean" because of his pessimistic outlook on the
world. He was not without his sense of humor, however.
Noting the ungracious, forbidding character of so many "good"
persons, and suspecting that many of them would be among
the ninety-and-nine just persons who need no repentance, he
said, "We who know them on earth can understand that their
appearance in Heaven will not be greeted with enthusiasm."

Our Father, give us glad faces, winning ways, the lovable aspect of faith, that will set men to rejoicing in thee. In the Spirit of Christ. Amen.

Week 12——Day 3 Read Rom. 15:24

"Be of good cheer," said Jesus. How can one *command* cheer? Is not joy one of the fruits of the Spirit? There is also a Christian duty of cheerfulness, whatever the circumstances. In 1884 Robert Louis Stevenson wrote to his father: "My cold is still very heavy, but I carry it well. Fanny is still very much out of sorts, principally through perpetual misery with me. I fear I have been a little in the dumps, which, as you know, Sir, is a very great sin. There is no more abominable sin than this gloom, this plaguey peevishness."

Despondency and faith hardly go together. But if joy is a most characteristic note of the New Testament why do we meet so many joyless followers of Christ? We cannot always control the melancholy moods that sometimes come, but we do not need to wallow in them. Herbert Farmer wrote: "The man who dallies with despondency dallies with evil and walks naked in the midst of his enemies."

Come, Lord Jesus, for in thy presence we will not dally with despondency. For thy sake. Amen.

Week 12——Day 4 Read Isa. 35:10

In his book *Applied Imagination* Alex Osborn refers to a Swiss gentleman who meticulously reviewed his eighty years on earth and calculated how he had spent them: twenty-six years in bed, twenty-one working, six eating, the same being angry. He frittered away five more years in waiting for tardy people. Shaving took up 228 days, scolding his children twenty-six, tying neckties and blowing his nose eighteen, and lighting his pipe twelve days. He added sadly, "I figured that I laughed for only forty-six hours in all my life!"

Trivial, irrelevant? Perhaps. But out of the knowledge that the God we see in Christ has entered our world to save it comes, not forty-six hours of laughter, but a lifetime of abiding joy.

We are not alone, O God, for thou art with us. In thee do we have our joy. In Jesus' name. Amen.

Week 12——Day 5   Read I Cor. 16:15-20

Sheppard and Marshall introduced *Fiery Grains,* their book of instructive excerpts from literature, ancient and modern, with this reminder: "There is an idea abroad among moral people that they should make their neighbors good. One person I have to make good: myself. But my duty to my neighbor is much more nearly expressed by saying that I have to make him happy if I may." We see from the close of nearly every one of Paul's letters that those of the earliest churches understood this duty. Do we understand it?

Show me this day, our Father, how I may make some neighbor happy. For Jesus' sake. Amen.

On May 24, 1738, John Wesley's heart was "strangely warmed" by his conversion. Paul knew that kind of experience: "Thanks be to God who delivers me." But read Wesley's *Journal* for October, 1738, five months later. He reports inner desires quite unholy, no love of God within himself, deadness and wandering of mind in prayer, cold inattention to communion. "I have not that joy in the Holy Ghost; no settled, lasting joy. Nor have I such a peace as excludes the possibility either of fear or doubt." Paul knew this, too: "I (still) serve the law of sin." It is a blessed thing to be converted, but let us never doubt the need for continual renewal in Christ.

Lord, deliver me from complacency over my conversion and defend me from despair over my sin. For Christ's sake. Amen.

Henry Drummond once told a large assembly of university students, "Gentlemen, I beseech you to seek the kingdom of God first or not at all. I promise you a miserable time if you seek it second." The truth of his words is attested by the people, of whom Archbishop deBlank reminds us, who have just enough religion to make them miserable. Their vision of God turns the world's rewards into dust and ashes. On the other hand, because they have never surrendered completely to the demands of God's kingdom they are denied the full joy of his service, a joy that always comes through pain, but a pain by which one finds the true meaning of his life.

Help me, O God, to make an offering to thee of that which hinders my seeking thy kingdom. Through Christ our Lord. Amen.

Though he slay me, yet will I trust him.—Job 13:15 (K.J.V.)

God and Our "Leftover Lives"

Week 13——Day 1   **Read John 16:32-33**

Caitlin Thomas, the widow of the poet Dylan Thomas, described the desolation of her life in a book called *Leftover Life to Kill.* The title suggests the despair every person feels in the valley of death's shadow. Jesus himself wept at the sadness of Mary and Martha when Lazarus died. He understood what it meant to find oneself with "leftover" life. Christian faith takes us beyond this, however. "If Christ be *not* raised from the dead" then we might have leftover life to kill. But "Christ has been raised from the dead to become the first fruits" not only of those who have died, but of all the rest of us who fear death. In him is not leftover life to kill but new life to live. In that faith one is able to say, "Though he slay me, yet will I trust him," both with what has been taken and with all that remains.

O God, let us not kill the remainder of life, but live it in the joy and hope of our risen Lord. In his name. Amen.

Week 13——Day 2   **Read Ps. 91:9-12**

"No evil shall befall you." Life makes such a mockery of those words! Hideous and appalling evil befalls men without regard to virtue or faith. But the words do not promise that we shall not suffer. The gospel promises quite the opposite—we shall suffer, and life rewards the righteous with a crown of thorns. The promise is that no ultimate evil shall come to the soul of one who hides his life under the shadow of the Almighty. May God keep us all when we pass through the terror. It is not sentimental. One place evil cannot enter to destroy is the place where we stand trusting God.

Father, we do not ask to be saved from the burdens of the world. Only help us to be strong to stand by thee when evil comes. For Christ's sake. Amen.

Week 13——Day 3   **Read Matt. 27:62-66**

Pilate tried to seal Christ in his tomb, but against the resurrection neither his soldiers nor his stones were of any avail. Before we scoff at Pilate's presumption suppose we have a look at ourselves. Do we never try to seal the Savior in his sepulcher? When we live more in anxious fear of death (as though Christ had not been raised) than in confirmed trust that our Father is not the God of the dead but of the living, is this not a "stone" to seal Christ in the tomb? When we revile or exploit any man, woman, or child for whom Christ died and rose again, is this not a mighty rock to seal Christ from coming with justice? When we cause the least of God's children to stumble and fall, missing their chance to walk in the newness of Christ's rising, is this not a wall against his coming? By these ways we try to keep Christ in his tomb. But he breaks out—and will release us from our tombs if we let him. In the power of the risen Lord we can find courage to let the stones be rolled away and trust him wherever he leads.

Raise us from death to life, our Father. Through Christ our Lord. Amen.

United Press International reports the word of The Sterling Silversmiths of America, an association of experts, that the best care one can give his sterling flatware is hard use. Surprising? They say that daily use makes polishing almost unnecessary and gives the metal a much desired patina.

Is the same not true also of our faith? The only way to keep its luster is to use it. A faith that is put away only to be used on great occasions first tarnishes and finally becomes unuseable. Are the great affirmations of God's judgment and love among the resources we will use this day? It will be better for them, and for us, if we take them out of the closet of our piety and give them some rugged use in the transactions of life.

O God, may we not hide, but use the gospel of Christ, that the most common purposes may have uncommon consequences. For Jesus' sake. Amen.

What some men will do to "know the truth"! The report appeared in the newspaper of four men who drifted two thousand miles across the Pacific, from California to Hawaii, on a raft. Devere Baker said, "I am not an adventurer, I merely want to know the truth. Our *Book of Mormon* speaks of travel across great oceans by raft. I wanted to prove this truth."

Each person must prove the truth he believes by demonstration of it. That it is more blessed to give than to receive; that only by forgiveness can the healing love of God bind up life's wounds; that in Christ Jesus there are no distinctions of color, class, or country—to know these truths try them, even at great risk. Jesus did, and he found that of God's faithfulness there was neither end nor limit.

May we continue in Christ's word, O God, and so know that truth that sets us free. In his name. Amen.

Week 13——Day 6 Read Ps. 46

It is reported that in some places, hard pressed by danger in World War II, *alarm* and *despondency* were punishable offenses. To disturb people's quiet strength by needless alarm or to discourage hope by either despairing thought or despondent action was against the common defense and security. The thought follows that to the Christian both alarm and despondency are not only against the common defense in a difficult time, but they are also unnecessary and contradictory to his faith. Alert and concerned about the life of our souls and our communities we will be, but with Almighty God our refuge and strength we will not cry havoc and we will not give up in gloom.

In all alarms we would know thy peace, O God. In our despondency lift us by thy grace to trust thee no matter what. For Christ's sake. Amen.

Week 13——Day 7 Read Luke 11:29-32

The eleventh is a disturbing chapter of Luke's Gospel to read, filled as it is with condemnation. There is good news here, too, but it is good only to those who have first faced the condemnation of Jesus' judgment. Something greater than Jonah is here. That is *good* news! Good, if we have taken the sign of Christ seriously. Are we not also a generation which seeks a sign? We want "proof" that Christianity will win over Communism, that righteousness will be rewarded. Faith comes not from signs but from trust in God's love beyond all guarantees, and frequently in the face of signs pointing to an opposite end. A sign has been given—Christ's resurrection. We are to trust it!

Grant us grace, O God, to trust where we cannot see, and believing, find all joy and peace. In Jesus' name. Amen.

The earth is the Lord's.—Ps. 24:1

Old Tales of Space and Time

Week 14——Day 1   **Read Heb. 13:8**

A recent book bears the title *New Tales of Space and Time.*
The stories which it includes are fiction, although they are
hardly more amazing than the new "tales" of space and time
that are true. Yet the old tale of space is still the most marvelous: "When I look at thy heavens, the work of thy fingers
. . . Go into all the world." The old tale of time is still the most
wonderful: "In the beginning God . . . Jesus Christ is the same
yesterday and today and for ever."

*Time bears us away before it is finished, our Father, and the
end of space is beyond our ken. But we do not fear, for thou
art God. We pray in the name of him whose spirit has gone into
all the world, and whose loving power remains the same now
and forever, even Jesus Christ our Lord. Amen.*

Week 14——Day 2   **Read Exod. 3:1**

God is not bound to one place as the early Semites believed.
It was hard for them to accept the truth of God's continuing

presence. No less difficult is it sometimes for us to be sure that as we move into new worlds of space, new circumstances of life, new concepts of thought, God does not remain attached to some older universe, some previous circumstances in which we have known him, some earlier scheme of thought. God's presence is in the "new" universe, the mysterious unknown, the painful circumstances.

Otherwise, O God, we would be forlorn of hope. We pray in the spirit of Christ. Amen.

Week 14——Day 3   Read Ps. 91:1-6; Rom. 14:8-9

Our minds are much occupied with thoughts of survival. Some have built fallout shelters; all are troubled to know how to survive should the day of nuclear adversity come. Our faith tells us that survival is more than physical preservation. Preservation for what purpose? Existence to what end? Life with what trust?

Build shelters we may or must, but the Christian will know that the primary question is whether he dwells in the shelter of the Most High. The primary need is so to live now that whether we live or whether we die tomorrow, we are the Lord's.

Bring us to abide in thy shelter and shadow, O God. Be thou our refuge and fortress. So may we live in highest confidence and holiest purpose. In Jesus' name. Amen.

Week 14——Day 4   Read Ps. 90:1-4, 16

Scientists now speculate that according to Einstein's theory if an astronaut were to travel *at or near the speed of light* he could (theoretically) journey to the Andromeda galaxy, 1,500,000 light years round trip, while he aged only 55 years. Time "slows down" at the speed of light. While he was gone, however, the earth would have aged 3,000,000 years! What was it the psalmist said, "A thousand years in thy sight are but as yesterday when it is past"?

Thou, O God, art neither earthbound nor the prisoner of time. Not by space travel, but by being in love with thee, lift us, if possible, from our captivity to the moment, that we may have some vision of eternity. In the spirit of Christ. Amen.

Week 14——Day 5   Read Luke 9:57-62

A fussy traveler was having much trouble in placing her belongings in the railroad coach. She put bundles first on the seat, then on the floor. She opened and closed windows, adjusted shades, and fidgeted about like a nervous hen. When her husband protested, she said, "I want to get fixed so I can see the scenery comfortable." He shook his head. "Susan, we ain't goin' far, and the scenery will be all over before you get fixed to enjoy it."

Many people go through life "getting fixed to enjoy it"— while life passes and is gone. Every day God's world is before us to see and enjoy. Pity the person who is too busy getting ready for some future and never sees the wonders of the present.

Lord, save us from blindness and fussing with ourselves, that we may see the wonder and glory of thy creation. In Jesus' name. Amen.

In ten other places the book of Proverbs commends the "fear of the Lord." There is a special meaning in this use of the word "fear," better expressed to our minds by "awe" or "holy dread." It is the feeling of amazement at the unimaginable holiness of God. As R. Gregor Smith recognized: "It transforms man's anxiety about himself and his world, leaving him with only this one fear—a trembling adoration of the transcendant Holy Lord." In this sense John Middleton Murry's word is true: "No man knows life unless he has been terrified by it . . . by the joys and beauties of life . . . the fact of birth as far more "awful" than the fact of death."

Let our knowledge begin in holy wonder and awe before thy greatness and thy goodness, O God. In Christ's name. Amen.

G. K. Chesterton wrote:

The miracles of the old world, such as the song of birds, the rushing of water and the passing clouds, remain miracles today as they were centuries ago, for all those who have eyes to see and ears to hear. But the rapidity in the wonderful inventions which we witness today is a rapidity in things going stale—a rush downhill to the flat and dreary world of the prosaic; a haste of marvelous things to lose their marvelous character, a deluge of wonders to destroy wonder.

Fill us this day, O God, with wonder at thy greatness, humility before thy love, obedience to thy will. Amen.

WEEK 15

Into thy hand I commit my spirit.—Ps. 31:5

He's Got the Whole World in His Hands

Week 15——Day 1   **Read Luke 23:46**

Few songs has Marian Anderson sung with more feeling or power than the spiritual "He's Got the Whole World in His Hands." The metaphor of the hands of God is sacrament of a saving and sustaining truth: It is both divine judgment and everlasting mercy to be in God's hands.

In one of the loveliest books of children's prayers Constance Bannister concluded a verse with the line: "Thank you, God, for Father's hand." On the facing page is a simple picture of a man's hand grasping the tiny hand of a child. Recall what Jesus says of his Father's hands, "My sheep hear my voice . . . and I give them eternal life . . . no one shall snatch them out of my hand." God's hands never let us go. Jesus thought in the final moments of his life of the wonderful hands of his Father. This thought can be support for us every day. God's hands are underneath all things, and into the keeping of his hands all things may be safely and surely committed, now and forever.

Help us, Father, to trust all life to the keeping of thy hands. In the spirit of Christ. Amen.

What a strange paradox: this verse, coupled with Jesus' words from the cross. D. H. Lawrence said, "It is a fearful thing to fall into the hands of the living God. But it is a much more fearful thing to fall out of them." How can God's hands be fearful yet wonderful at the same time? The psalmist speaks of God's hands being *heavy* upon him. John Donne opened this truth for us: "Even upon his own children God's hands shall grow heavy, but that heaviness shall awake them. . . . In prosperity God's hand grows heavy for our not having employed our temporal benefits for their right use." God's hands are always heavy and fearful when they forbid us from evil. Thank God for his fearful hands. They save us.

Put forth thy hand, O God, to restrain us from wrong and lead us into truth. In Jesus' name. Amen.

Luke included the wonderful story of the blind beggar (Mark tells us his name was Bartimaeus) not just to show how full of compassion Jesus was, though that would have been reason enough. The evangelist must certainly have intended that everyone who ever heard the episode told would recognize himself in Bartimaeus, blind to so much that we would and could see. To every Bartimaeus, blind in heart or spirit, Jesus asks, What do you want me to do for you? He asks it of us. Do we want sight for faithful living, heart for generous service, courage for fearless confession? What do you want Christ to do for you?

Lord, we ask thee to open our eyes that we may see the wonders of thy love and the needs of thy world. Through Jesus Christ our Lord. Amen.

Week 15——Day 4 Read Matt. 6:7-8

In one of her lovely *Sonnets from the Portuguese* Elizabeth Barrett Browning protested her love to her husband:

> I love thee to the level of every day's
> Most quiet need, by sun and candle light.

Most blessed is any wife or husband whose partner loves him or her to the level of each day's quiet need—the needs we never utter but keep in the inner recesses of our being, yet where they are not hid from sensitive and loving imagination. Most blessed are we also in assurance that God, our heavenly Father, who is more sensitive and loving than we can even imagine, loves us to the level of each day's need—all the needs of this day. Neither do we need to shout or whisper them to him; he knows them. But we tell him even as we give thanks that he knows.

We need to be loved by thee; we need to love thee back, our Father. Thanks be through Christ that both are possible. In Jesus' name. Amen.

Week 15——Day 5 Read Ps. 38; Luke 10:17-20

As Sherman's army cut its devastating way across Georgia a slave woman watched the seemingly endless line of marauding soldiers. After a while she remarked: "I don't suppose they've all got names!" It is easy to understand her feeling. James Baldwin's *Nobody Knows My Name* is a book about people living today in a depersonalized urban society. It gives vivid stress to the truth that loneliness is the peculiar mark of our time.

Jesus said, "Rejoice that your names are written in heaven." What a fine way to put it—God knows our names, each one an individual loved for his own sake. The psalmist prayed with hope because he had confidence that God knew and cared about him.

If our names are written in heaven, they ought also to be written on earth. If God knows our names we ought to know each other's names.

Praise be to thee, O God, that our names are written in thy heart. Help us to write each other's names in our hearts. For Christ's sake. Amen.

Week 15——Day 6   Read John 6:63; Phil. 2:5

Rufus Jones called to mind Emerson's observation that if you hold a straw parallel to the Gulf Stream the ocean will flow through the straw. It is true also that when a life comes into parallel direction with celestial currents the divine Spirit will flow through it. Jesus has spoken to us words of life; when we hold ourselves parallel to his trust, to his compassion, to his obedience, we find the same divine Spirit flowing through us, even as it flowed through him. In grief God's abiding love can uphold us; in perplexity God's greatness can sustain us; in fear God's encouragement can steady us—if we hold ourselves open to the inflowing of his Spirit.

The tide of thy Spirit rises within us, O God. We will fear nothing which this day may bring. In the name of Jesus. Amen.

Week 15——Day 7   **Read Luke 8:40-48**

"Some one touched me." These are wonderful words, for us no less than for the woman who in the pressing throng touched the fringe of Jesus' garment. They say to us that when we reach out in faith to receive help from our Lord he does know. Just as the Master felt the slight tug of a frail woman's hand upon his robe, though he was then being jostled by a throng, so God is aware of every appeal to his mercy. He is never so beset by a crowd, or a world, as not to feel the touch of your hand.

O Lord Jesus Christ, Son of God, have mercy upon me. Amen.

WEEK 16

If I be lifted up.—John 12:32 (K.J.V.)

There's a Comfort of Not Running Away

Week 16——Day 1   **Read Dan. 3:8-25**

Out of this great story in Daniel comes reinforcement for us in our need. In the fiery furnace of persecution for righteousness' sake a man can walk and not faint because one like the

Son of God walks with him. In the fiery furnace of penitence, surrender to God's love and atonement for sin, a person can endure the shame because one like the Son of God is beside him. In the fiery furnace of renunciation, where some cherished illusion or fond indulgence is given up, one can live with the denial because one like the Son of God does not forsake him. Says a character, who refuses to run from persecution, in Galsworthy's *The Mob,* "There's a comfort of not running away." The comfort is of him who ran not from his own cross, nor from ours.

If we have the comfort of thy going with us, we are strong enough, our Father. In Jesus' name. Amen.

Week 16——Day 2   Read Eph. 2:14-18

The refugees from East Germany have built a high cross just inside the boundary of West Germany. William L. Shirer wrote: "Each day, as the sun starts to go down, the shadow of the cross will move eastward unimpeded across the formidable line of the Iron Curtain- reminding the oppressed that there is hope." It is not quite clear from this image what kind of hope Shirer is talking about. But the symbol is clear that the shadow of the cross has moved across all the dividing walls of hostility which men have built against each other. Christ died for us all; within and beyond our opposition is a love in which we all have access to the Father.

We thank thee, God, that the shadow of the cross falls upon all, testament of thy love for all men on both sides of every wall. In Christ Jesus we pray. Amen.

I do not have to hide from the ugliness of the world, escape from the pain of sin, or refuse the loneliness of death by seeking distraction. This cup, by God's grace, I may drink to the dregs—because God is at my right hand. In his strength no evil is too frightful to face, no pain too sharp to support, no separation too awful to abide. God's strength is more than equal to all my needs. In the nights and days when despair clutches at my feet to draw me into the mire, let me remember *God at my right hand holding me up.* In the rush of temptation to sweep me into terrible, irrevocable acts, let me remember *God at my right hand holding me back.* On the high, steep slopes of lonely vigil and solitary climbing, let me remember *God at my right hand holding my faith.*

I thank thee, God, that against storms of temptation and the undertow of difficulties I need never stand in my strength alone, for thou art ever beside me to give thy support. Through Jesus Christ. Amen.

A famous Dutch altar piece shows a crucifix hanging on the wall at the back of the Bethlehem stable. What a strange mixing up and running together of the events of Jesus' life! An anachronism—to have the image of the man's death involved with the joy of his birth? It is, however, as Stephen Hopkinson commented, a paradox full of meaning. There are stern realities at Bethlehem. The nativity involved a humiliation—the Son of God casting away his glory to take upon himself the form of a humble servant, obedient unto death.

Our Father, in the gracious humility of our Lord's birth, let us never forget the appalling humiliation of his death; but finding in that death the evidence of thy steadfast love, may we discover also the true joy of his coming. Amen.

Week 16——Day 5   Read Luke 5:12-16

Lepers were untouchables. According to Levitical Law a leper must cry, "Unclean! Unclean!" wherever he went, warning people to shun his presence. Lepers were the most lonely and rejected of all men. But verse 13 of today's scripture tells us that Jesus touched the leper. The Master, in William Barclay's words, always touched the untouchable and loved the unlovable. And so must we.

The passage is a consolation as well. There is no uncleanness within us, whether of body or soul, flesh or spirit, upon which Christ will not lay healing hands.

Master, we know thou wilt heal us, if we will allow thy touch upon our hearts. So may it be even this day. For thy name's sake. Amen.

Week 16——Day 6   Read Isa. 35:1-2

Above Hoover Dam in Arizona is a plaque and flagpole—memorial to the men who lost their lives in the construction of the dam. Inscribed thereon are the words, "They gave their lives that the desert might bloom." Thousands of square miles of southern California have blossomed through irrigation from the Colorado, and life has been made brighter and better by the power generated at Hoover Dam. That the desert of our lives might also blossom, in safety, in joy, and in love, many have given their lives.

Our Father, keep us mindful of the price others have paid that our lives might be full of light, peace, and joy. For Christ's sake. Amen.

Week 16——Day 7   Read Luke 15:1-10

Until he finds it! That is how far the shepherd goes in search of the one lost sheep. His is no quick glance about the hillside and then home to the ninety-nine. Hunting for lost sheep was no safe or easy affair in ancient Judea. Danger, quite commonly death, awaited the man who ventured into the wilderness. But the shepherd went, and for just one sheep! He went until he found it. We remember this day the Good Shepherd who goes to the limit of earth's wilderness to find us where we are lost and to bring us home.

O God, whose purpose it is to seek and to save every one who is lost, turn us to repent. Then grant us a share in heaven's joy; through the Good Shepherd who gave his life for us. Amen.

WEEK 17

*Let us . . . lay aside . . . the sin
which clings so closely.—Heb. 12:1*

Laying Aside the Purple

Week 17——Day 1 **Read Heb. 12:1-2**

When the Emperor Constantine was baptized shortly before
his death he "laid aside the purple and passed away in stain-
less white." One might point out that such "death-bed piety"
is not very convincing. Nevertheless, wonderful suggestion
comes from that picture. We can take it to mean for ourselves
laying aside the things that interfere with doing God's will and
serving God's justice. What garments of personal preferment do
I wear in my family life? What coverings of self-righteousness
do I flaunt before others? In what robes of violence and false
accusation do I contend against my neighbor?

*Lord, thy kingdom is ever at hand. Help me to lay aside
those things which prevent its advance. For Christ's sake.
Amen.*

Week 17——Day 2 **Read Matt. 13:24-30**

Two suburbanites surveyed their lawns across the split-rail
fence which divided them. Jokingly they counted the heartily
detested dandelions in each other's grass. Whereupon one asked
of his friend, "Which way does the wind blow?" In other
words, would the seeds take wing from Harry's lawn into Joe's
yard, or blow from Joe's weeds onto Harry's grass? A far more

87

serious question we all might ask is, Do evil seeds blow from my language or example into the good grass of someone else's life? Were we to look at Jesus' parable from "behind the scenes" we might hear it say to us, Be careful what evil seeds you sow in the good soil of another's life!

Let me keep my life from hurting any other. In the spirit of Christ. Amen.

Week 17——Day 3   Read Matt. 7:13-14

Douglas Steere tells us, "I once saw a heavily loaded truck stuck in an underpass. There could be no getting through short of unloading. I was reminded that the way is still narrow and the gate is still straight that leads into life." What are the things we must "unload" if we are to enter the life of which Jesus speaks? Is it an undue attachment to possessions? Is it an insistence upon personal comfort at all cost? Is it indulgence in some habit, defense of some prejudice? We'd better examine the load we're trying to take through with us. Some of it will have to be left behind.

Show me what it is, O God, that keeps me stuck in the way to life and help me to leave it behind. For Jesus' sake. Amen.

Week 17——Day 4   Read Gen. 4:1-5

Edward Rowland Sill in *The Fool's Prayer* has put in poetry the truth that it is "by our follies that so long we hold earth from heaven away."

"Hard, well-meaning hands thrust among the heartstrings of

a friend . . . ill timed truth we might have kept . . . the word we had not the sense to say."

The writer of Genesis tells us, "Cain was very angry." But he wrote about us. What things we do in anger that destroy our brothers! Sometimes we make murder polite—but our brothers' heartbreak cries to God from fields and houses of destruction.

Rebuke us for our jealousies and selfish angers, thou God of judgment. Be thou merciful to us and to those we have hurt. And heal us by thy love. For Christ's sake. Amen.

Week 17——Day 5   Read Exod. 20:4-6

Children of the Ashes is the revealing title of a book on the rebirth of Hiroshima. Vividly does the author, Robert Jungk, light up the ancient truth that "the iniquity of the fathers is visited upon the children to the third and fourth generation"— not in the commonly imagined sense of a petty, pouting God, but in the terrible moral sense that evil leaves in its devastating aftermath. In times when we grow weary of the frustrations in peacemaking it is both sobering and salutary to remember all who died in the wars of the world's evil, to feel our shame that man's sin (our sin!) should have exacted such sacrifice, and to pray that by God's mercy we shall visit no comparable con-demnation upon the generation yet unborn.

We pray this day for peace, O God. Enlarge the hope for peace by the remembrance of the cost of war. In Jesus' name. Amen.

In his book *Something Went Wrong* Lewis Browne wrote of the Belgian Congo:

The natives were literally hounded to death. Forced labor, forced migration, recurrent pillage destroyed half the population in 15 years. But one of King Leopold's exploiting corporations made a profit of 1800 per cent in four years, a second 1700 per cent in six years, a third yielded the king a personal income of $1,500,000 a year.

Something was very wrong. Should we wonder at the reckoning of God's judgment for man's abominations against man, in the Congo and everywhere on God's earth where men have not been their brother's keepers?

O righteous God, let us not think that we can escape thy reckoning. Through Jesus Christ who is both Judge and Redeemer. Amen.

Some years ago Edna St. Vincent Millay wrote words whose truth is timeless:

Over a period of many years we have been growing steadily more and more lax in our deportment, both private and public; more and more slovenly in our ethics. Those of us who do not commit crimes, condone them in others. . . . It is that which is killing our country! How can we put a stop to it? . . .

Are you a Christian? Do you call yourself that? Then you know what to do to please Christ. You know the kind of person to be to make him feel less sad. Be, then, the kind of person of whom he can be proud. Do, then, the things that would please him.

Grant, Lord, that we give thee no cause this day to be ashamed of us. For Jesus' sake. Amen.

WEEK 18

Giving thanks always for all things.—Eph. 5.20 (K.J.V.)

Giving Thanks in a Shipwreck!

Week 18——Day 1   **Read Acts 27:27-44**

Giving thanks to God—in the middle of a shipwreck! How many of us would have done it? More likely we would have been found crying for help at the lifeboat station, as were some sailors on Paul's ship. This was Paul's secret: *He always gave thanks to God.* Their good fortune had been amazing, they had food to give them strength for the ordeal; they had prospects for rescue. Having received so much, Paul must give thanks. It could have been either gratitude or panic. With gratitude is not only the way Paul lived, it is also the way he would have been found if death came.

Bless the Lord, O my soul, and despite every storm, forget not all his benefits. Through Jesus Christ our Lord. Amen.

In early New England it was the custom at Thanksgiving to place five grains of corn at every plate as a reminder of the first winter when food was so depleted that only five grains of corn were rationed to each individual at a time. The Pilgrim Fathers wanted their children to remember the suffering which made possible the settlement of a free people, to remember that on the day in which their ration was so reduced only seven healthy colonists remained to nurse the sick, and nearly half their numbers lay in the "windswept graveyard" on the hill, that when the "Mayflower" sailed back to England in the spring, only the sailors were aboard. It would help us, not only at Thanksgiving but continually, if we kept visible some reminder of the price that has been paid for us.

Discipline my imagination, O God, to see my bounty compared to the meager fare of those who made the way for me. In Jesus' name. Amen.

Theresa of Avila in the sixteenth century wrote of rights that are wrong:

Fly a thousand leagues away from saying, "I was in the *right;* it was not *right* for me to suffer this way; they had no *right* to do such a thing to me."
Now God deliver us from such wrong rights! Do you think that there was any question of rights when Jesus suffered the injuries which were so unrighteously inflicted on him? . . . When we receive honors or affection or kind treatment let us think what right

have we to them—for certainly we have no *right* to them in this life.

To think with gratitude is to shift gears from dwelling upon our imagined rights to wonder at our incredible blessings.

Our Father, do we take any things for granted as our rights which have come only through thy grace or someone's love? One right above all others we would claim: The right to praise thee. Through Christ our Lord. Amen.

Week 18——Day 4   Read Job 15:11

The consolations of God! Amid sufferings and denial do we consider anywhere nearly enough the consolations God offers? Hope for some success or achievement may have failed, but it remains that "we are the sheep of God's hand," that he does not forsake us, even the least or the last of us. We may have been cowardly and done inexcusable things, yet God says to us still, "Go in peace; your faith has saved you." We may have lost the earthly presence of one who was the joy of life, nevertheless God promises still, "He that believes in Christ shall never die."

These are the consolations of God. They compensate for everything else, and nothing can take them away.

We thank thee, God, for thine infinite patience with us, and the everlasting mercy of thy love. Through Jesus Christ our Lord. Amen.

Henry Sloane Coffin once wrote of the grace of thankfulness:

Let us scan our circumstances for causes of gratitude. Take the worst—the saddest occurrence of the year, the bitterest cup that was pressed to our lips, the most tragic loss—and as one looks it over there are always mitigating elements, things that might easily have been far more distressing, circumstances connected with it for which one cannot help being sincerely thankful. And along side the occasional tragedy place the blessings which have come to every one of us—home happiness, love and friendship pouring their unstinted joys, far more kindnesses shown us than we have merited, the discipline of life, God's forgiveness and His healing grace.

Bless the Lord, O my soul! And forget not all his benefits. In Jesus' name. Amen.

"Fail Safe" is the code name given to the safety system which has been established so that a nuclear attack could not accidentally be launched by this nation. An exciting novel by that title has brought the system to peoples' prominent attention. The words suggest another meaning to be found in the New Testament. Christian faith has built into it a fail-safe assurance. One can fail and yet be safe in the love of those who confess Christ and safe in God's mercy. The compulsion always to succeed is removed. Christ came to call those who do not always succeed. This brings reinforcement to all people who are beaten out in life's severe competition. It also helps the person who knows that to love God, whatever the consequences, is more important than to win the prizes of this world's competition.

Praise and thanks be to thee, O Father, that our failures never separate us from thy love nor hinder thee in thy healing. In Jesus' name. Amen.

Week 18——Day 7   Read I Cor. 4:6-7

Try making a list of things that are yours that were not given but which you earned by work or merit. *Your job?* Many people work hard, put the best they have into a job, but what job is there that does not depend on the sacrifice and cooperation of colleagues? *Your mind?* Most of us apply ourselves to acquire knowledge, but what of all who patiently taught us, zealously labored to communicate what we could not understand? *Your health?* Have you taken care of yourself? What of all the family and public efforts at hygiene, preventive medicine? *Your character?* We discipline ourselves to stand above moral reproach, but what of all those whose persuasion and love restrain us? And who could merit or earn the love of family and God? What do I have that I did not receive as a gift?

We neither make nor belong to ourselves. All that we have is a gift, O God. Thanks be to thee. Through Christ our Lord. Amen.

Keep the charge of the Lord your God.—I Kings 2:3

King David—Loyal to the Royal in Himself

Week 19——Day 1   **Read I Sam. 17:31-49**

Our meditations this week will take us through six great moments in the life of David. To dwell thoughtfully upon the Old Testament psalmist-king may be to find both secret and strength for our own faithful living.

David's reply to Goliath, "I come to you in the name of the Lord of hosts," brings encouragement to every person who finds himself in David's situation—unevenly matched in resource, experience, reputation. David came in the name of the Lord. That makes a powerful difference, although it does not always guarantee victory. Note also that David went up with confidence and courage, remembering the strength God had given him in times past and trusting him for that strength now.

Let us go against every foe of the good life in confidence that in thy name is power, O God. For Christ's sake. Amen.

Week 19——Day 2   **Read I Sam. 24**

Michelangelo's great statue shows David in the supreme moment of his youthful courage before Goliath. What a companion statue he might have done of David in his supremely magnanimous moment when with Saul in his power he would not lift his sword in revenge! Although Saul had tried to kill him, David was generous toward the disturbed king when he could have taken his life. Is David's magnanimity not instructive for us? Are not the people who give us provocation to revenge really the "lord's anointed" against whom we are to stay our hands from violence or hurt?

O Lord, we would not put forth our hand in revenge against any of thy children. In Jesus' name. Amen.

Week 19——Day 3   Read II Sam. 1:17-27

David's lament for Saul touches deep chords of appreciation; we admire his respect for his king and his acknowledgment of Saul's earlier greatness. His lament for Jonathan plays upon the even deeper chords of friendship and grief. "Your love to me was wonderful," he exclaimed. Neither kings nor crowns, nor thrones nor empires, could hold the place in David's heart that belonged to Jonathan. David made great mistakes in his life, but never the mistake of missing the value of friendship. To have fine friendships is to be wonderfully blessed.

Lord, let us keep our friendships from neglect, and let us be worthy to be called friend. In Christ's name. Amen.

Week 19——Day 4   Read II Sam. 6:12-19

These verses describe one of the notable moments of Israel's history—bringing the Ark for the first time to Jerusalem. But notice how David brought it—rejoicing, dancing with all his might, shouting, leaping, to the sound of the horn. Here was no heavy solemnity, no funereal gravity, but joy! To have the

Ark of the Lord, with all it symbolized of God's promises, was reason for rejoicing. Something is woefully lacking in anyone's religious faith and experience if it does not move him to "dance with all his might" out of sheer joy.

Release us from foreboding fear and inhibiting self-concern, O Lord, so that with all our might we may praise thee. For Christ's sake. Amen.

Week 19——Day 5   Read II Sam. 12:1-14

Thank God for Nathan—that he found David out! Indeed, David caught, shamed, condemned, became David the penitent, heartily sorry for his misdoings. (Read it all in Ps. 51.) David getting away with his sin, putting it over on one and all, might never have been moved to repent. It may seem harsh at the time, but there is a salvation in being found out; it is a good thing that sin does not usually stay hidden from common sight. Is it not a reminder that no sin is *ever* hidden from God's sight?

Lord, we have sinned. Defend us in the shame of discovery, and enable us to put away all hurtful things. In Jesus' name. Amen.

Week 19——Day 6   Read II Sam. 18:24-33

No cry in all the Scriptures or in all the recorded words of mankind comes out of greater depth of anguished pain than David's lamentation for his son Absalom. What a great man we see here—wanting to die himself in the place of his traitorous son! Moved to the depth of his being, the second time death had robbed him of a son, David walked through the valley of the shadow. He is our companion when we must pass the same way. It helps to walk in steps he has taken.

Sustain us in every grief, O God; as thou didst uphold thy servant and king in the far-off days, so bear us up through the same hours that time does not change. In Christ's name. Amen.

Week 19——Day 7   Read I Kings 2:1-4, 10-11

What a pageant of life passes through memory as we see David in the hour of his death—courageous before Goliath, magnanimous toward Saul, friend of Jonathan, joyful before God, penitent and forgiven after sin, full of love for his son, and crowning it all, through all and in all, a magnificent faith. "Keep the charge of the Lord your God," he admonished his son, Solomon. This was the wish with which he died, as it had been the precept by which he lived. The admonition still holds; there shall not fail us a man who walks in God's ways.

We would walk before thee in faithfulness, O God, with all our heart and soul. In the Spirit of Christ. Amen.

WEEK 20

What Do You Put in First Place?

Week 20——Day 1   **Read Matt. 19:16-22**

A friend of Turgenev once wrote to him, "It seems to me that to put oneself in the second place is the whole significance of life." To this the great Russian author replied, "It seems to me to discover what to put before oneself in the first place is the whole problem of life." A prophet of ancient times saw that problem when he asked what the Lord requires. He saw the answer, as much for us now as for his own time and people: To walk humbly with him. What you put in first place makes all the difference.

Life is torn, our Father, as we try to put ourselves ahead of thee. We are humble to think that we can have any place with thee. Through Christ our Lord. Amen.

Week 20——Day 2   **Read Matt. 22:23, 34-36**

We have no record that the Pharisees ever asked Jesus a question for the purpose of learning anything. They questioned him repeatedly, but always to make their own point. Quite aside from their malicious motive, what a sad spectacle—no curiosity, no openness to receive any truth that might conflict with their prejudice. Someone has said, "The pleasure of ignorance is the pleasure of asking questions. The man who has exchanged it for the pleasure of dogma—the pleasure of answering

—has already begun to stiffen." Only the person with the humble mind before the truth will ever learn from the truth, or learn even what the truth is.

O God, may we ask even more than we answer and listen more than we speak; so teach us and lead us into greater truth.

Week 20——Day 3 Read Matt. 7:6

A young American woman stood before Beethoven's piano in a Vienna museum. Presently she struck off a few discordant notes.

"I suppose," she said to the attendant, "that many noted musicians have inspected this instrument."

"Oh, yes," replied the man. "Recently Paderewski was here."

"Paderewski!" exclaimed the visitor. "Certainly he must have played something wonderful."

"On the contrary; he did not feel worthy to touch it."

Our Father, have we this day like swine trampled under foot that which is holy—any offering of soul, any testament of beauty, any appeal of need? Forgive us. Through Christ our Lord. Amen.

Week 20——Day 4 Read Prov. 22:1-16

Many years ago a student challenged President Francis Wayland of Brown University who had spoken of the great wisdom of the Proverbs. Scoffed the student, "I don't think there's anything very remarkable in the Proverbs. They are rather commonplace remarks of common people."

"Very well," said Dr. Wayland, "make one." The student beat an embarrassed retreat. Ancient wisdom must always be examined in the light of new truth, but our own presumption is rarely an adequate test.

In humility help us, O God, to stand judgment before the insights and wisdom of ancient peoples, who feared thy justice and reverenced thy faithfulness. In Jesus' name. Amen.

Week 20——Day 5   Read Ps. 43:2-5

One day George Eliot said to Herbert Spencer that considering how much thinking he did she was surprised to see no lines in his forehead. He replied, "I suppose it is because I am never puzzled." She was shocked and said, "That is the most arrogant thing I have ever heard." It is also one of the most pathetic things a man could say of himself. Never puzzled before the mysteries of creation? Never outraged by its contradictions? Never baffled by its ambiguities?

O God, save us from being cocksure of thee or arrogant about what we know. Humble us before the divine mysteries; then lift us up in faith. Through Jesus Christ. Amen.

Week 20——Day 6   Read Jer. 2:35-37

It is strange that we should expect to be sustained by powers which the Lord has already rejected. Israel put her trust in Egypt and Assyria. But God had rejected them, and they could not save her. Does the gospel leave any doubt that God has rejected money, privilege of any kind, and all the idols of

102

man's power as instruments of our salvation? Yet we continue to trust them!

How long, O Lord, will we put our trust in the things which thou hast rejected? Turn us and teach us to love that which never fails because it is of thee. In Christ's name. Amen.

Week 20——Day 7 Read Acts 4:9-12

Barrett Wendell wrote in 1919: "Historically considered, the gospels tell the story of a remarkable man, who lived under extremely fixed earthly circumstances, remote from any we know, and died before he was old enough to have much experience." Jesus—not much experience of life? When we look at what men have done in the world with all their knowledge and experience would we not sooner pray with George Matheson to the Author of life:

Son of Man, thou never growest old to me. Last century is old. Last year is old, last season is an obsolete fashion, but thou art not obsolete. Thou art abreast of all the centuries; nay, thou goest before them like a star. I have never come up with thee, modern as I am. Amen.

What does the Lord require?
You shall love the Lord your God.—Deut. 6:5

Putting Life on Center

Week 21——Day 1   **Read Ps. 46:1-3, 10**

For many of us the chief problem in life is to have a life that is
not scattered and pulled and thrown to the four winds, but a
life that is "on center," single in its devotion although varied in
its interest and occupations. Charles Morgan has given us a
beautiful figure of speech when he described "the stilling of the
soul within the activities of the mind and body, so that it might
be still, as the axis of a revolving wheel is still." When life
"centers down" in God we may be the still axis within the revolving wheel of relationships, obligations, and activities.

*Center us down upon thee, O God, so that all our affairs may
hold together and have thy will as their purpose. Through Jesus
Christ. Amen.*

Week 21——Day 2   **Read Deut. 30:15-20**

At a junction in Arizona is a huge sign: Left—Albuquerque,
Right—Los Angeles. If you have business in either place it matters greatly which road is taken. Life continually brings us to
the dividing ways of blessing and curse. We must choose life
or death for the mind—stretching for the fine things, the hard
tasks, or contentment with cheap, easy occupation; life or death
for the soul—locking our souls in the prison of ourselves, or

flinging them out to God and to people. Often at the time these choices are made it seems to make little difference what we do, even as the first miles on either road at the Arizona junction are much the same. But in our choices for the mind and soul we turn into a road that leads either to life or to death. *Loving the Lord your God means life.*

O God, from the beckoning maze of highways let me choose this day a way that will bring blessing to someone, and so follow further upon the road that leads to life. For Christ's sake. Amen.

"Aliens in a land belonging to others." Stephen here refers to Israel's bitter sojourn in Egypt. One who tries to be faithful must *always* live as an alien in a land "belonging" to others. Among people who would make race or class or religious creed the criteria by which the worth of a person is judged we ought to be aliens. In a society where wealth accumulates but men decay the Christian is an alien. To a way of life that worships power above compassion we will be either aliens or apostates of Christ. It is easier to be altogether "at home" in the world, but the world can be redeemed only as men serve a citizenship in a kingdom that is not of the world.

Keep us, O God, from loving the world so much that we are aliens in thy kingdom. In Jesus' name. Amen.

Francois Mauriac had this to say about exclusive love:

If we want to know in what relationship we really stand to God we cannot do better than to consider our feelings about other people . . . particularly when one person above all others . . . is the source of all our happiness and all our pain. If our peace of mind depends upon him alone, then, let it be said at once, we are separated as far from God as we can be, short of having committed mortal sin.

The Genesis story is a dramatic way of saying this. The point is not that God would ask any man to murder his son. Rather that we offer our fondest human loves to the greater love of God.

O Lord, let us not love our loves the less, but thy love the more that all love may be toward thee. For the sake of Jesus Christ our Lord. Amen.

Antoine de Saint-Exupéry said,

Sacrifice is the gift of oneself to the being of which one forms a part. Only he can understand what a farm is, what a country is, who shall have sacrificed a part of himself to his farm or country, fought to save it, struggled to make it beautiful. Only then will the love of farm or country fill his heart. A country—or a farm—is not the sum of its parts. It is the sum of its gifts.

Truly said! And only when one has truly sacrificed for God's sake will he know God, and the love of God fill his heart.

We love thee, our Father, because of thy gifts to us; we know thee more truly by our sacrifice for thee. In Christ's name. Amen.

Week 21——Day 6   Read Acts 3:1-6

In Ignazio Silone's novel *Bread and Wine* Marta says to Nunzio, "This ring is my birthday present to Don Benedetto." Replies Nunzio, "My dear lady, you make your brother a greater present every day . . . You have made him the gift of every single day of your life."

With such a gift to God no other can compare.

We would give thee the best we have—the days of our years—gladly and in fullest measure. Use them, and use us, for thy name's sake. Amen.

Week 21——Day 7   Read Mark 4:14-20

Will Durant says of Pope Leo X, pontiff of Rome in 1517 when the Reformation burst full force from the Roman Catholic Church: "All his faults were superficial except his superficiality." What a devastating indictment! But have we not known such people? Theirs are not gross sins of the flesh, nor yet mortal sins of the spirit. Peccadillos, we might say, except what may be a most frightful sin—superficiality itself. And we ourselves—are we reasonably "good" people, but superficially committed Christians, loving God with only a heart's fraction?

Lord, have mercy upon us for skimming the surface of life and not plumbing the depths of devotion. In Jesus' name. Amen.

107

WEEK 22

I hold fast my righteousness.—Job 27:6

Fidelity Outranks Inspiration

Week 22——Day 1   Read Ps. 119:169-76

The composer Peter Ilich Tchaikovsky once wrote in his diary: "Worked without any inspiration, but successfully." We all do that. God uses our uninspired work for this purposes. He has to. We depend for our very lives upon what people do for us in uninspired moments. Is the jet pilot constantly "inspired," or the doctor, the superintendent, our husband, or our wife? How could we expect unfailing inspiration from human beings? Yet upon the "success" of what they do our lives depend. Fidelity outranks inspiration among the marks of the Christian life.

Give me understanding of thy word and will, O God, and let me be faithful no matter how I may feel. For Jesus' sake. Amen.

Week 22——Day 2   Read Job 27:6

Jonathan Swift once said, "I have never been surprised to find men wicked, but I have often been surprised to find them not ashamed." This points to what Joseph Wood Krutch has called *the new immorality.* There has always been wickedness among men, but never until now have so many apparently accepted and taken for granted personal dishonesty; saying, in effect, "Everybody does it, and besides, I can't see that it really hurts anybody."

How often do we say, quite unconsciously, "Everybody does it; it can't be very wrong"? Job kept his integrity—would not compromise what he believed to be the truth. Wrong is still wrong no matter how many may call it right.

Keep us always alert, O God, that we judge ourselves not by popular opinion, but by thy Word. Through Jesus Christ our Lord. Amen.

Week 22   Day 3   **Read Matt. 5:37**

Van Wyck Brooks once observed how many New England "Yankees" had become what Matthew Arnold called "Philistines" when they were subjected to complex social conditions that tended to cheapen their minds, in contrast to the relatively simple life by which they had thrived. Not being able to live up to those new complex conditions without discarding *moral ballast*, they were tempted to throw over the certainties and the standards by which they had once lived so securely and to compromise their minds with the taste of the world.

This is a danger ever present to all Christians—discarding the moral ballast by which life is kept steady and true in order to go with the popular currents. No life can be altogether simple, but dropping moral ballast is to court danger on high seas.

Help us, our Father, to say yes to right and no to evil without compromise of thy will. In Jesus' name. Amen.

Week 22——Day 4   **Read I Cor. 10:12-13**

From Lisle Bell comes this remarkably prophetic word: "Until there is a run on his moral capital, no man can measure the strength of his banked resources of courage." Thank God most of us are spared a disastrous run on our moral capital. Yet we take foolish chances; we allow our minds to entertain thoughts of possible infidelities, half persuading ourselves a fraud would go unnoticed, resorting to easy half truths in all kinds of daily commerce. Paul's word is wisdom: "Let any one who thinks that he stands take heed lest he fall." "Mad Anthony" Wayne, who fought the Indians in the Northwest Territory, had a memorable maxim: "A good general is never surprised."

Merciful God, grant that we may never so carelessly expose ourselves to evil that we shall be surprised by our fall. For Jesus' sake. Amen.

Week 22——Day 5   Read Mark 8:36-37

About six years ago the Department of Commerce discarded some of its old files. Amazing things were found in these abandoned files—countless instant coffee jars, most of which were empty; rubber gloves; rubber boots; books of all sizes. Among the books was a Bible. Not consciously or deliberately, but how revealing of our life—a Bible discarded by the Department of Commerce! Does it not speak in symbol of the way much of our commercial life has discarded the Bible, and along with it the knowledge: "What does it profit . . . to gain the whole world and forfeit . . . life?"

Have we discarded the Bible from the ordering of our affairs too?

God, we would remember that in getting and spending we lay waste powers that should be put in the service of love. In Jesus' name. Amen.

During World War II the Nazis tried repeatedly to persuade Richard Whittington-Egan to "collaborate" with them in the occupation of conquered European countries. All they asked him to do was broadcast over the radio saying how well he was treated. In return they would make life easy for him and his suffering wife. Unlike some of his younger compatriots he scorned the offer. Though tired and hungry he would not follow the multitude to do evil. He kept his integrity at dreadful price, but it was his finest hour.

Thanks be to thee, God, for brave souls who held righteousness dearer than comfort. May we follow in their train. Through Christ our Lord. Amen.

"Thus Esau despised his birthright." He held his inheritance cheaply, lightly dismissed his wonderful heritage. It is one of the most tragic scenes in scripture. What a sobering sight!

What are we doing with our birthright? Some of us had the blessing of a wonderful home, a mother and father from whom we received a birthright of integrity and generosity. What are we doing with these? We all share a national birthright of freedom from our forefathers. How about that? In Christ we received a birthright to suffer for a broken world and to witness to God's love for that world. Have we despised or cherished that birthright?

Keep us ever true to every great inheritance that is our right to claim, our Father. Through Christ our Lord. Amen.

Guard what has been entrusted to you.—I Tim. 6:20

Keeping the Securities of the Faith

Week 23——Day 1   **Read I Tim. 6:20-21**

James Moffatt translated this verse: "Keep the securities of the faith intact." If Paul were writing today he might see the analogy to a man's financial capital—as did Jesus in talking of the *talents*. How does one keep his securities intact? By investing them and by using them. Foolish is the man who puts his money in a mattress. The only way to have it is to invest it where it will be wisely used to keep its present worth. The same applies to the securities of the faith—forgiveness, mercy, trust in God. To keep these we must use them; to have them we must every day invest them in life.

Help us, O God, to guard what thou hast entrusted to us, not by hoarding it, but by investing it in life. For Jesus' sake. Amen.

Week 23——Day 2   **Read Luke 18:18-30**

These verses contain hard sayings. Surely they do not mean that a person must irresponsibly walk out on his home and family to be a vagabond Christian. Jesus cared too much for family love ever to want that; he was obedient to his own parents through the years of his youth and young manhood, and when he died he kindly gave his mother into the tender care of his beloved disciple. The verses must not be "explained away," however. Everything we have must be given to the kingdom of God—nothing held back for private employment. This means all that we have, even home, family, vocation—all these must serve the purposes of God's will.

The Victorian painter George Watts put this life motto on his seal: "The Utmost for the Highest." For whatever, or Whoever, is highest nothing less than our utmost and best will do. And that from which we withhold our best cannot be highest for us.

Our Father, forbid that we should hold anything back from serving thy purposes. Show us how home and work, play and service, may contribute to thy kingdom. For Jesus' sake. Amen.

Week 23   Day 3   Read I Kings 21:20-29

One ought to read the whole chapter—the story of Naboth's vineyard. Ahab sold himself to do a base thing, but God is not mocked. After Nora Waln's anti-Nazi book, *Reaching for the Stars* was published Heinrich Himmler, Hitler's executioner, seized seven children as hostages. He then told Nora Waln he would release them and as many other people as she could list on a large sheet of paper if she would promise to write nothing further about Germany except romantic novels. She declined, saying, "If you make a bargain like that, God takes away the power to write. If you don't tell the truth, you lose your talent."

Lord, let us not sell ourselves to untruth of any kind, especially the untruth of betraying the best which thou hast put within us. For Christ's sake. Amen.

The word "cumber" appears twice in the King James Version of Luke's Gospel: Martha was "cumbered with much serving," and the barren fig tree "cumbereth the ground" in Jesus' parable. To be cumbered is to be fruitlessly used up, vainly burdened to distraction. From Ivor Brown's book, *Having the Last Word,* comes the surprising information that in Westminster Abbey is a statue to Saint Uncumber! She was the benefactress of wives, uncumbering them of evil husbands. We may not believe in the ministering power of saints, but the name of this unusual saint suggests our continuing need to be uncumbered from that which uses us up in vain without return to God.

Uncumber us of our many vanities, our Father, that we may have time and devotion for thee. In Christ's name. Amen.

There is a sense in which every person ought to live a divided life—not, of course, divided in the great loyalties of his life. In these a man's eye ought to be *single* in its devotion. But many persons fail properly to divide the important from the inconsequential, the eternal from the transitory. Many things we cannot escape doing; they are the stuff of daily existence. In Christ, however, a person should find perspective on these things, learn to do them with his left hand, so to speak, without getting altogether absorbed in them. Our great energies and devotion should go to the great purposes of God's kingdom. These we divide from the chaff of necessary but secondary trivialities.

Help us, O God, to put the things that are first with thee first with us and to serve them with the best we have. In the Spirit of Christ. Amen.

Week 23——Day 6   Read Luke 16:1-2, 11-12

The National Bureau of Standards has developed a camera capable of taking such tiny photographs that it could record the entire Bible on a small part of a penny. Remarkable? Imagine it—the entire scriptures on a fraction of a cent. This is hardly new, however. Many ministers and church treasurers will testify that people have been doing that for years. Some people have condensed the entire message of the Bible to the measure of a penny. The gospel has called forth a penny's worth of commitment; everything Jesus said about stewardship, being faithful in the use of what is God's, is contained in a penny. We should not need magnification of 1250 times to get the message!

Help us to be generously faithful in using what is not ours, but thine. In Jesus' name. Amen.

Week 23——Day 7   Read John 17:19

Of the first battle of Bull Run, Bruce Catton wrote, "What really turned MacDowell's battle into a defeat was something that happened in the Shenandoah Valley a few days earlier." These are provocative words. A failure by General Patterson to immobilize the forces under Joseph Johnston, fifty miles from Bull Run, meant defeat for MacDowell's Union Army.

How often this is true—failure to keep a trust, loss of courage, the search for an easy way out may have severe consequences for others a long time or a far distance away. Especially does our everyday behavior have crippling consequences for our children.

O Lord, help us to be true to all sacred trusts, inconspicuous and obscure though they be. Then let us leave the issue in confidence with thee. For Jesus' sake. Amen.

WEEK 24

The fruit of the Spirit is . . . peace.—Gal. 5:22

Clear of the Brooding Cloud

Week 24——Day 1　　　　　　　　**Read Matt. 17:1-8**

The Romance of Mountaineering by R. L. G. Irving contains a striking photograph showing the incredible massif of Mount Blanc in France. Dark clouds completely envelope the middle slopes, but the ultimate peak towers high into the blue sky. "Clear of the Brooding Cloud" reads the caption beneath the picture. So does any mount or moment of transfiguration take us clear of the brooding cloud. By communion with God the brooding cloud of anxieties and limitations is left beneath us for a time of renewal at the heights of heaven.

From the heights above the clouds of earth may we hear thy voice, O God, feel thy hand, and know thy love. Through Christ our Lord with whom we may climb the steep ascent toward thee. Amen.

Peter, James, and John went above the brooding clouds of earth to a transfiguration. But they had to come down from the Mount. Jesus would not have them building booths in which to linger for a long time. Transfiguration does not last indefinitely; hard duties await us at the foot of the Mount. The Son of Man (and his followers!) will suffer. If the communion above the brooding cloud has been real, however, we do not need to fear the return to the shadows. Christ enters into every dark place with us, and the gift of his Spirit is peace.

Come with us, O God, through days of suffering and shadow, demands and duty, waiting and work. For Jesus' sake. Amen.

G. K. Chesterton has given us wonderful words to ponder: "The peace given in the churches is less attractive to the religious spirit than the war promised outside. For one man who wants to be comforted, a hundred want to be stirred. Men, even ordinary men, want in the last resort not life or death, but *drums.*"

The man of Christian faith, confident that nothing can hinder God's saving power, listens eagerly for drums. Possessed of an inner peace which the world can neither give nor take away, he waits for drum and trumpet to summon him to the service and mission of God.

If we march to the drum beat of thy call we have the life which is life indeed. In Jesus' name. Amen.

John G. MacKenzie points out that memory can be a guardian angel as well as an evil spirit. A well-stored mind is a mighty resource against days of great demands. Poetry lovers will call upon their favorite passages, lovers of travel their happy recollections, bereaved souls will substitute for their sense of loss gratitude for the long years they had their loved ones. If each day or each week we add some treasure to the mind it may sustain us in the hard days by way of reminder. When the time comes, as it does so continually for many, when all is dark and no treasure is to be had, we may feed upon the reminder of what God has done for us in Christ. He has broken down every wall of separation between ourselves and him. In this reminder there is peace.

Great peace is ours, O God, when our minds are stayed upon truth, beauty, and goodness that are not withered or shaken. Through Christ our Lord. Amen.

Samuel Taylor Coleridge wrote in his *Aids to Reflection:*

The first step in spiritual experience is neither the search for intellectual certainty, nor submission to authority; it is quite simply to hunger and thirst after righteousness, to be aware of a deep sense of personal infirmity, and manifold imperfection, and to feel accordingly, the want, the necessity of religious support . . . . In short, whatever *finds* me bears witness for itself that it has proceeded from a Holy Spirit.

Let me be aware of my needs, my Father. Then will my hunger and thirst for thee bear witness to the presence of thy Holy Spirit. In Jesus' name. Amen.

Arthur Gossip points out that most people believe because someone they know gave them convincing demonstration of the faith. Leo Tolstoy in describing how he came to grow from pessimism to conviction tells us: "I saw around me people who, having this faith, derived from it an idea of life that gave them strength to live, and strength to die in peace and joy."

Would anyone grow to conviction from looking at our lives? Does our whole being—all that we are and do and say—call out, "Come, and I will tell what God has done for me. He has not removed his steadfast love from me"?

Thanks be to thee, O God. Help me to declare it wherever I go. For Christ's sake. Amen.

In his helpful book of devotional resources, *Leaves from a Spiritual Notebook*, Thomas Kepler quoted this from Louis Bromfield:

I was tired in the head and in the spirit. Now I think it came partly from never being alone, because in the world in which I lived nobody ever seemed to want to be alone. They seemed to have a terror of it. They all wanted to lunch together, or play golf together, or go to the country club or women's clubs together, or meet in the hotel bar or in the corner drugstore to kill time over the pinball machines. On their tombstone will be written, "He lived without ever being alive. Nothing ever happened to him."

Unless my help comes from thee, O God, I am living but not alive. Come each day to my aloneness and keep my life. In Jesus' name. Amen.

The fruit of the Spirit is . . . kindness . . . gentleness.—*Gal.* 5:22

Footnotes to Faith

Week 25——Day 1   **Read Ps. 150**

It was said of D. W. Brogan that in his book *Politics in America,* "On every other page he drops footnotes, which, unlike most footnotes, are even more sprightly than the body of his text." Sometimes the footnotes of life are the joy of an otherwise solemn text of existence. An unexpected kindness, an unprompted remembrance, a joke, a song, a light in the eye, a squeeze of the hand—these are little touches that add sprightly documentation for a profound faith. How about adding a footnote to faith and love for someone this day?

We thank thee, O God, for the faith that allows us our gaiety. In Christ's name. Amen.

Week 25——Day 2   **Read Eph. 4:31-32**

Life levies a crushing toll upon us all; tensions we cannot relieve, conflicts we cannot resolve, questions we cannot answer, mysteries we cannot explain, duties to which our strength is not equal, demands we cannot meet, sorrows that break our hearts, disappointments that break our hopes. As one man put it, "Most of us are in trouble." Kindness does so much. The remembrance of how life is hurting someone else and our response of gentleness, the encouraging word spoken to one passing through the season of dismay, the thoughtful gift to someone who imagines that he is forgotten, the happy surprise to a person who may have almost forgotten how to smile, the considerate silence concerning one who is ashamed, the forbearing loyalty to one who has failed—these give life.

Let all malice be put away, our Father, and may we be kind to one another. Through the Holy Spirit of Christ. Amen.

Week 25——Day 3   Read II Tim. 4:9-10

He was a man of wise perception who observed, "Every man is the prisoner of his talents." A talent for persuasive promotion may keep this man from caring about what he promotes. A talent in some field of fashion may keep this woman from recognizing real beauty. The gift of easy speech many people have made the substitute for hard thought. On the other hand, some have been lifelong captives to a talent for generosity, kept alive by the renewing influence of the Holy Spirit, whose gift is a sensitive imagination and a disposition toward kindness.

Constrain me, O Lord, by thy Holy Spirit that gentleness may be my way and kindness the bond that tethers me to all men. In Christ's name. Amen.

Week 25——Day 4   Read John 11:28-36

"Jesus wept." That is the shortest verse in the Bible. Two words—but what volumes they speak, what comfort they contain! Jesus wept; he understood our sorrows, he was touched with the feelings of our infirmities. Out of his sharing of the troubles that come to us all he was able to help.

In Thornton Wilder's play *The Angel That Troubled the Waters* the angel says to the man beside the pool, who can never reach the healing waters when they bubble up, "In love's service only the wounded soldiers can serve." This is so because the person who has been wounded, by the kindly moving of the Holy Spirit, can feel with all other wounded.

Enable us, merciful God, to use our discouragements and distress in the service of love. For Jesus' sake. Amen.

Week 25——Day 5   Read Acts 20:28-31

Again and again Paul, in letters to all his churches, spoke of the ministry of encouragement. We live in a lonely world, a world filled with all kinds of fears. Is there any more priceless gift we could give each other than the gift of encouragement? The encouragement of support—we may be able to uphold someone in his discouragement. The encouragement of confidence—to someone timid about himself we may give the confidence to believe in himself. The encouragement toward the best—for the sake of another we may put ourselves under the discipline of the highest. The encouragement of warmth and joy in the kindness of the Spirit may make all things new in the heart of another.

Gracious God, who hast encouraged us, may we also give much encouragement to others. In Jesus' name. Amen.

Week 25——Day 6   Read Mark 5:25-34

In this passage we see how Jesus was aware of people and their needs even in the midst of a throng. Harlan Miller reminded us that people's looks are misleading as we see them apparently bent on trivial errands. In the jostling crowd is a boy headed for the draft board, a new widow, a woman seeking a divorce, a man with an incurable disease, a little girl with a toothache, a lonely girl going to meet a stranger, another girl going to the confessional, a couple trying to borrow money, a family picking out a casket—on and on goes the procession of trouble and pain. Jesus would recognize it in our day as in his.

O God, let our spirits be kindled by the kindness of Christ till, seeing with eyes of imagination and sympathy, we become aware of the needs which his eyes would not miss. In his spirit. Amen.

Week 25——Day 7   Read Ps. 69:16-20

The story is told of a woman who was left a widow fairly young in life. Having to earn a living, she put an ad in the paper saying that she was willing to listen to anybody talking to her about anything at all for $2.50 an hour. Her scheme was such a success that within two years she had a staff of almost fifty people just listening to others! This is a caricature; it may be apocryphal. But it reminds us that the world is full of people such as the psalmist who need the comfort of someone just to listen.

Open our ears that we may hear with understanding and empathy, our Father. In the Spirit of Christ. Amen.

WEEK 26

The Lord of hosts is with us.—Ps. 46:11

Staying Power

Week 26——Day 1   Read Eph. 6:10-17

William E. Hocking once wrote:

The difference between one man and another is largely a difference of *staying* power; staying power cannot be tested in the laboratory, except in minor ways. The whole outcome of a battle or of a campaign may depend on what a few men will do when their "backs are to the wall"; but the situation of being at bay cannot be reproduced in the testing room.

Not reproduced, but anticipated. We know the day of real testing will come. We can gird ourselves with resources and prepare by the practice of faith to stand in that day. The Lord of hosts is with us and in his strength we shall be able for all things.

May we never be taken by evil's surprise, nor caught with mind and soul depleted of thy resource, O God. For Christ's sake. Amen.

Week 26——Day 2   Read Luke 5:17-26

"Rise, take up your bed and go home." These words Jesus spoke on a day long ago in Galilee. The same words he speaks to us on this day. To someone paralyzed by prejudice Christ says, "Arise from these rigidities of mind that keep you from

124

entering a life of new understanding and relationships." To someone bound by injurious habit Christ says, "Arise from this slavery that keeps you from a new life of service and commitment." To someone bound by sin Christ says, "Arise from your sin and guilt and be forgiven, and be free."

Christ says these things because in the power of God's love he can do them for us.

In amazement at thy power and thy love we glorify thee, our Father. Through Christ our Lord. Amen.

Week 26 —— Day 3   Read John 11:25-26

Albert Schweitzer once said that the supreme tragedy in life is outliving yourself. People sometimes continue their physical existence after the inner life of their souls is dead. The death of genuine feeling, the death of inspired response, the death of the awareness that makes it possible to feel the pain or the glory of other people in yourself—this is really to die. But to trust life to the leading of God in Christ—this is to stay alive all your life, even unto everlasting life.

May we be born anew each day to thy purposes which give eternal life to our souls. For Christ's sake. Amen.

Week 26—— Day 4   Read Ezek. 24:15-18

There is saving instruction for us in verse 18 of this chapter. Ezekiel said that his wife died in the evening, the desire of his eyes taken from him at a stroke. In the morning that followed he returned to his duties to do as he was commanded. This was his heroic way of facing grief. Sorrow and tears there were—for these are the tokens of love—but the prophet must face the tasks appointed to him, grief or no grief. Having a duty to perform takes from the mind a "rooted sorrow," distracts the heart from faithless brooding. Knowing that bereavement will come to us all, it is good to resolve in advance that we will carry out what is commanded of us. It is our way of continuing integrity toward the one we have lost and toward God.

In loss as in gain, in death as in life, command us, O God, and grant us the will and courage to obey. For Christ's sake. Amen.

Week 26——Day 5   Read II Sam. 12:15-23

In this great story note especially verse 20: "Then David arose. . . ." Lee Clair Libby once said of this, "Here is a portrait of a great king." Out of his grief David arose, dressed in his royal clothes, went to worship, and took up again his kingly tasks. Never do we see David in an act of greater character. To every one of us will come a day of profound grief such as David passed through. Then it may be that with God's help we can arise in our sorrow, resume the tasks to which life has called us, and with the face of kingly consecration go on with God's appointment to life.

Lord, thou wilt be gracious to us in grief. In thy providence appoint us to such tasks as we dare not refuse. In Jesus' name. Amen.

T. A. Kantonen put a central truth in commanding words: "Other religions and philosophies may teach continuity through immortality. The Gospel teaches responsibility through resurrection." There's the difference. Now that Christ is raised from the dead we have entered a new life of responsibility. *In the keeping of his commandments* the Holy Spirit comes to abide with us forever. In his presence we discover the staying power for the responsibility which he asks. In that responsibility is new joy and new life.

By thy Holy Spirit may we find the responsibility of the resurrection for us. In the power of him who is our Risen Lord. Amen.

The Lord gives us one day at a time. All he asks is that we live faithfully *that one day*. Yesterday is in his keeping; tomorrow belongs to his providence; and this day he is with us. In his upholding I can bear whatever the day brings. God asks not that we cross all the bridges of the journey on one day. One by one the days come; one by one we pass through them. Trusting that God will fill my cup to the level of each day's need, I will live this day in faith, as though it were my last, and as though it were the first of a great succession. But only this day—today.

As my days so shall my strength be from thee, my Father. In Christ's name. Amen.

But God.—Ephesians 2:4

Inside the Borders of the Possible

Week 27——Day 1   Read Judg. 6:11-14

John Buchan wrote in his dedicatory letter to the mystery thriller *The Thirty-Nine Steps* that he has an affection for "the romance where the incidents defy the probabilities and march just inside the borders of the possible." That's a great place to march and to live. It seems improbable that jealousy and ill will could be overcome by love, but God puts this change inside the borders of the possible. A person may think that death or failure has robbed his life of any future joy or gladness but in Christ he finds these inside the borders of the possible.

Because thou art with us inside even the most narrow confinements of our lives, our Father, let us in confidence expect the wonderful to be possible. In the Spirit of Christ. Amen.

Week 27——Day 2   Read Acts 2:24

But God. . . . This gospel is full of the most astonishing reversals and recoveries. Just when life has weighted the equation against us God appears with astounding power and strikes victory into the heart of defeat. Life does terrible things to us; we suffer broken hopes, moral failures, profound denials. *But God* is able to bring forth good out of evil, even the appalling evil of what the world tries to do to him. *But God* is able to bring forth light out of darkness, even the darkness of sin. *But God* is able to bring forth life out of death, even the death of the cross.

We are cast down in much doubt and evil; but thou, O God, art able for our every need. Through Christ. Amen.

Week 27——Day 3   Read II Cor. 7:6

The same two words, *But God.* Whenever I am threatened by some event that would shake my purpose, destroy my integrity, move me to acts of shame, rob me of courage, I need some reinforcement from beyond myself. The more I dwell on the peril the more disconcerted I become. M. V. Dunlop suggested a technique of renewal. I may say to myself, "No, I will not accept my feeling from this event. I will draw it from thee, Spirit of holiness within me. And in the joy and peace of knowing thy power of holiness is with me, I will deal with this situation."

My feelings, O God, let them come not from any threat but from thee. So may it be, through Jesus Christ. Amen.

Week 27——Day 4   Read Rev. 11:15-19

The difficult yet wonderfully inspired book of Revelation speaks of final things, God's ultimate victory over the powers of darkness and evil. Sometimes it speaks in the present tense: "The kingdom of the world *has become* the kingdom of our Lord." But has it? Rome fell, but other empires have risen. Truly the end is not yet, but even in the present God has demonstrated his power, which is above all earthly power. There is goodness and love even in the kingdoms of the world which will continue in the *omega* of God's kingdom. We wait, we pray, and we live with all hope and all confidence.

Even so, come, Lord Jesus, and let thy Spirit dwell in us now and forever. Amen.

Week 27——Day 5   Read John 16:32, 33; 17:15, 24-26

In the narrative which accompanied the amazing films of Col. John Glenn's flight aboard *Friendship* 7 the commentator said, "Col. Glenn is now on his journey toward the night of tomorrow and the dawn of yesterday." He made reference to Glenn's passage through three "days" of sunrise and sunset in four hours of earth "time." The words are prophetic; we are all on such a journey. Tomorrow will bring its nights of doubt and sorrow, but God's love has been declared for us from the foundation of the world. So in the power of what was revealed in the dawn of yesterday, we can face whatever tribulation the night of tomorrow may bring. In the world we shall have tribulation, but Christ has overcome the world.

Thanks be to thee, O God. Amen.

Week 27——Day 6   Read Heb. 12:1-2

F. D. Maurice once said of Thomas Carlyle, "He believed in a God who lived till the death of Oliver Cromwell." This surely must be unfair to Carlyle. Yet it comes uncomfortably close to describing the faith of many. Substitute some other name for Cromwell, associate the collapse of faith with some loss or adversity and the statement stands. "He believed in a God who lived till the last war." "She believed in a God who lived till her health failed." "He believed in a God who lived till Freud, Darwin, and Einstein."

Our Father, we are surrounded by a cloud of witnesses who believed in thee through all things. Let us with them look to Jesus and keep faith. For his sake. Amen.

Week 27——Day 7   Read Isa. 43:1-3

On Monhegan Island, off the coast of Maine, is a tiny grave: *Phoebe Starling—d. 1784—age 1 month.* All memory of this life has disappeared from the earth. Who knows her name now? Who cares any more that such a child ever lived, that she was ever loved, and that at her death was ever mourned? The answer is God! God calls Phoebe Starling by name. He knew her before she was born. He knew her when she died on that lonely island. God calls each of us by name. He remembers us. We are not forsaken to be alone in life. And at the hour of death God speaks our names.

I thank thee, our Father, that we are neither forgotten nor forsaken. Through Jesus Christ our Lord. Amen.

Even there thy hand shall lead me.—Ps. 139:10

Which Way Is Heaven?

Week 28——Day 1   **Read Ps. 139:11-12**

An article by David Greenfield describing the strange, dark immensities of space asks the question, "Which way is heaven?" Up, down, across, or far within? In the endless dark of outer space where is heaven? Earth becomes a tiny speck among billions of specks. Where now is the God whom we knew in the environment of sunshine and beauty and comfort?

Long ago the psalmist, knowing nothing of a universe of "space," nevertheless knew the vastness of the dark. He feared he might be lost in some dark, as awesome to him as outer space to us. Yet a great faith gripped him and held him: "Even the darkness is not dark to thee." Even the darkness of space is not dark to our God.

O Thou, whose light no darkness can put out and no space diminish, shine in all the dark and through all the distance of our lives. In Jesus' name. Amen.

Week 28——Day 2   **Read Ps. 46:1-3**

A cartoon showed a man and a woman at a counter marked "Educational Toys." A clerk was showing them a box filled with odd-shaped fragments and saying, "It's designed to prepare children for today's complex world. No matter how they put it together it doesn't come out right."

Beyond the humor there is truth here. It is part of our training for life to learn that things do not always "come out right." Only on television do the good guys always win. In this complex world goodness suffers injustice, kindness is abused, love is forsaken, and faithfulness is crucified. What we can learn from faith is that though even the earth be removed, God is with us. To serve and love him is its own reward no matter how things "come out."

Prepare us to love thee always, our Father, and to find in thy service both reward and refuge. For Christ's sake. Amen.

Week 28——Day 3   Read II Sam. 7:22

Do you have any Ebenezers around your house? Better get some reminders of how God has helped in the days of life's journey already passed. How God has helped! In the home where we grew up, in the religious inspiration that settled the course of our lives, in the love of companions that sustained us along the way, in the gift of children, in the forgiveness of so much by so many, in the great hopes which we cherish and the great loyalties which we serve—without these gifts what and where would we be? We had better keep some visible reminders before us—pictures or symbols which say: Remember how God has helped.

Hitherto hast thou helped, O God. Thou wilt help us still. For Jesus' sake. Amen.

133

On angry seas where they thought they would surely drown the disciples cried out in fear. Jesus came, and their fears were gone. Is it not a parable for us? When life finds us above frightful depths—in the desolation left by death, where sin eats away the soul itself, in the face of terrifying anxiety—Christ comes with his upholding, "Take heart, it is I; have no fear." The love of God is equal to all our needs. Storms have risen against us, but Christ comes across the water saying: "Take heart. . . . Come."

In the power of faith, O God, give us grace to walk where Christ calls, even over great depths. For his sake. Amen.

"He has visited and redeemed his people." G. K. Chesterton once said, "Nothing is real until it is local." That thought opens up great avenues for wonder and exploration. Death is never wholly real to us until it is local. So it is with suffering, sin, forgiveness, joy—all life's experiences. Salvation, the saving power of God, is not real until it is local, immediate to us, personal. God is real to us because he is local; that is, he has visited "locally" to redeem his people—us!

Help us to know the coming of thy love to our local needs, our Father. In the Spirit of Christ. Amen.

"If I make my bed in [hell] . . ." God is there. Praise him for that assurance! If most people are to find God anywhere today it will be in hell—the hell of our broken communities, the hell of our unspeakable nightmares of destruction, the hell of being lost from God. You usually expect to find God, not in hell, but in heaven. The good news of the Christian faith is that God has come into the very midst of our hell to love us, to find us here, and to lead us home.

Find me, O God, in whatever hell I find myself, and lead me through. For Christ's sake. Amen.

Week 28——Day 7   Read John 20.17-18

"Do not hold me," said Jesus to Mary Magdalene in the dawn of Resurrection Day. Mary must not *retain* him; rather she must go and prepare the disciples for the Master's coming with the Holy Spirit. The admonition is well addressed to us. It is wrong to try to hold Christ at any point of our meeting with him. He must always lead us into new and higher truth. Former ways change; we must know him in new relationships, new obedience. So it must also be with our own dead. They come back "in spirit" to console us, to lead us, but ever into new and larger ways of service.

Father, let us not try to hold either the risen Lord or the dear and holy dead. Let them rather lead us closer to thee. In the Spirit of Christ. Amen.

WEEK 29

Grow up . . . into [Christ].—Eph. 4:15

I Mean to Begin Again

Week 29——Day 1   **Read Mark 15:22-39**

In the memoirs of Edward Burne-Jones it is related that a young artist of considerable talent one day visited the studio of the great painter. With his customary courtesy Burne-Jones showed her his pictures. The two artists lingered for a time in delightful talk over the art which they both so dearly loved. When they returned to the drawing room the young artist was asked what she intended doing with her art. "I mean," she replied very simply, "to begin again."

When one has stood for a long enough time beholding the cross on which the Prince of Glory died it is impossible to come away without saying, "I mean to begin again."

May the contemplation of his cross, and our lifting of the same burden, show us what we really are and what we really do to thy love, our Father. Let this discovery stir us to begin again. In Jesus' name. Amen.

Week 29——Day 2   **Read II Cor. 5:16-17**

Some people think that the lobster of North Atlantic waters is nature's greatest gift to the human palate. This denizen of the cold ocean can be edifying as well as edible. Consider him (or her): "Lobsters grow in size only when they discard their shell. In the first year this occurs eight times, five during the second, and three times in the third. After that the male sheds twice a year and the female once."

Not a bad idea for us! To discard the shells of outworn prejudices, defensive reserve, and inhibiting selfishness—only thus can a person grow. The old self passes away so that a new one may be born in Christ.

Help me, Lord, to cast off the shells that keep me from growing in Christ. For his sake. Amen.

Week 29——Day 3   Read Mark 14.27-29

In a motion picture of rare beauty, *Whistle Down the Wind*, a fifteen-year-old girl comes upon a fugitive murderer hiding in a barn. Circumstances unrelated to her discovery lead her to believe the bearded man is Jesus. The criminal does not tell her who he is but begs her not to tell anyone of his presence. She gladly assures him that only the children know, and they won't tell. "You're safe with us . . . the grown-ups won't treat you this time the way they did before."

Is Jesus safe this day with you? Will you betray him or forsake him to another crucifixion before dawn tomorrow by faithless fear or by vain pride?

O Christ, may you be safe with us this day. And may the children of the world be safe with you always. Amen.

Week 29——Day 4   Read Acts 17:22-31

O Christ, you are a judgment upon our world. Even now, before the day fixed for God's judgment, you judge our adulteries by your purity, our hardheartedness by your compassion, our

137

excuses by your faithfulness, our dishonesty by your truth, our anxieties by your peace, and our sins by your forgiveness. There is mercy in your judgment, even as your judgment is itself a mercy, for in you we see both our need to be saved from our own worst selves and God's power to save us.

So may it be, our Father, through the resurrection of our Lord Jesus Christ. In his Spirit. Amen.

Week 29——Day 5   **Read Matt. 16:24-25**

In his *Age of Anxiety* W. H. Auden made confession for us all:

> We would rather die in our dread
> then climb the cross of the moment
> and let our illusions die.

By what illusions do I try to avoid the crucifixion demanded of a follower of the Crucified? The illusion that in the moral life I can reap figs from thistles? The illusion that I can cast off the burden of my sin myself? The illusion that God offers me cheap grace in some bargain basement dispensary?

Crucify my illusions, O God, that they may not keep me from knowing thee and finding in Christ the way, the truth, and the life. For his sake. Amen.

Week 29——Day 6   **Read Matt. 13:14-17**

Louis Nizer told this story as an illustration of perspective. On the opening night of *South Pacific*, Molly, the seamstress, could not be consoled in her tears. "The show's a flop," she told Mike Todd.

"Are you crazy? This is the biggest thing that ever hit Broadway."

But Molly insisted. "I stood out front for a while and watched. I tell you, Mr. Todd, you can see every seam in those dresses."

This was her department; we can understand her feeling. But what a lesson in perspective! It is so easy to miss the great meanings in life while we fuss over its seams.

Our Father, open our eyes that we may see thy works and behold thy glory in the face of Jesus Christ. Amen.

Week 29——Day 7   **Read Rom. 6:5-11**

There is no expressway to eternal life. We cannot part company with Jesus as he starts up the hill toward Jerusalem and plan to meet him in the garden on Easter morning. The only way to the resurrection is through another garden called Gethsemane. It leads over a high hill called Calvary. If we have died to ourselves with him, going his way of life and death, then we shall rise out of our former selves into new life. If we have used the stripes of suffering to heal the hurts of sin, then we are united with him. We are even now making our way to the resurrection.

O God, rescue us from dead ends and detours. Let us find thee now and go all the way to the resurrection with thee. Let our life and our death and our rising be like that of Jesus. Through Christ our Lord. Amen.

WEEK 30

Repent, and believe in the gospel.—Mark 1:15

Anonymous Evil

Week 30——Day 1   **Read Eccl. 12:13-14**

W. R. Matthews, one-time Dean of St. Paul's, London, put a truth that grows ever more timely:

Today, more than at any other period of history, men do evil without knowing clearly what they are about. We perform so many things by corporations, companies and committees. Most things of importance are done in our world by collections of people, and most evil is done in this way. The most appalling feature of modern sin is its dreadful anonymity. If we would be free from evil, we must know what we do.

This is an imperative truth to remember for it does not set aside the affirmation that God will bring every deed into judgment with every secret thing, whether good or evil.

Give us a right judgment in all things, our Father. Through Jesus Christ our Lord. Amen.

Week 30——Day 2   **Read Acts 2:37-39**

An advertisement for a home organ headlines the claim: "So easy to play you can enjoy it without lessons." The pitch continues: "No tedious scales and finger exercises before you can play real music. You sit right down and play." Has the age of automation brought us to the day when hard work, long practice, and demanding discipline are no longer required of one who would play music? It seems questionable. But is this not in the temper of our time? And in the life of the spirit, too? The first word of the gospel is still a hard and tedious demand: *Repent!* There is no way to succeed as a Christian without really trying.

Lord, move us to repent, turn from our ways and seek thy way. In Christ's name. Amen.

Week 30——Day 3   Read Mark 1:14-15

A cartoon showed a rhinoceros charging two hunters. One was reading to the other from the guide book: "Application for renewal of licenses will normally be made ten days prior to expiration date of old license. This requirement may be waived only in cases of extreme emergency. In such cases a letter explaining the circumstances in detail will accompany the application."

A charging rhino but fifty feet away would seem to be an emergency more extreme than any which had been imagined. The word is, Shoot! From the ridiculous to the sublime, the extreme emergency of the kingdom of God being at hand calls for drastic action. The word is, Repent and believe!

Let the time be fulfilled for us, O God. May we yield to thy kingdom's coming this day. For Christ's sake. Amen.

Week 30——Day 4   Read Gen. 3:8-13

Adam blamed Eve, who blamed the serpent. Passing the buck of responsibility is as old as Eden. "It's not my fault," we protest as we hurry out of one of the side exits of responsibility. Arnold Toynbee has given us words to ponder: "One of the perennial infirmities of human beings is to ascribe their own failure to forces that are entirely beyond their control. This mental maneuver is particularly attractive to sensitive minds in periods of decline and fall."

Am I guilty, O Lord? Do I pass the buck and shift the blame for my failures? Help me to look at myself first and repent before I blame others, or society. In Jesus' name. Amen.

Week 30——Day 5   **Read Prov. 15:1-7**

Good medicine for the soul it is, however discomforting, to consider from time to time what folly our mouths have poured out—and be chastened! Lord Byron once called Shakespeare "a damned humbug." Horace Walpole said of Dr. Samuel Johnson, "I cannot imagine his reputation will be very lasting." Emerson disposed of Charles Dickens, "His eye rests always on surfaces; he has no insight into character." Of Shelley, the sage of Concord remarked, "He is never a poet." These prophets judged only themselves in their foolish utterances. How often have we hurt others by harsh words or folly of judgment?

Let us not render cocksure judgment against anyone to his hurt, nor darken counsel without wisdom. For Jesus' sake. Amen.

Week 30——Day 6   **Read Job 42:1-3**

Said the *Harrisburg Patriot and Union* of Lincoln's Gettysburg Address: "We pass over the silly remarks of the president;

142

for the credit of the nation we are willing that the veil of oblivion shall be dropped over them and that they shall no more be repeated or thought of." Out of their own mouths they condemned themselves! But is it not a sin we all need to confess—hasty and ill-considered judgment meted out, often to someone's serious hurt? Recall some of the absurd and unkind things you have said to "hide counsel without knowledge."

Forgive us the sin of unmerciful judgment, our Father; the dogmatic certitude whereby we make fools of ourselves and unfairly estimate the worth and intention of others. For Christ's sake. Amen.

Week 30——Day 7   Read Acts 3:11-16

Six Characters in Search of an Author is the title of Luigi Pirandello's best known play. The title comes strangely to mind in reading Peter's sermon. "You killed the Author of life. . . ." Is it not a fair description that each of us is a character in search of an Author? The Author of life is God; he would put us into his plot—make us part of his purpose—but we pass him by, turn away from the roles in which his Son would cast us as witnesses, fishers of men. This is the way we kill the Author of life, we refuse to be his characters in the working out of his will.

O Lord, be thou the Author of every part we take in the affairs of life, so may we find ourselves as servants of thy will. For Jesus' sake. Amen.

In everything . . . with thanksgiving.—Phil. 4:6

Lend Me a Dream

Week 31——Day 1   **Read Num. 12:5-6**

A. C. Spectorsky tells of the worried exurbanite on her way to her psychoanalyst who stopped at a neighbor's house to plead, "You must help me. I'm on my way to my analyst's and I haven't dreamed anything. Lend me a dream." *Lend me a dream.* Someone else's dreams would not help the psychiatrist with me. But the dreams of others have helped *me.* I borrow them when my vision is low, the dreams of those who have dreamed great things about God and about men. I have discovered that dream becomes reality when we act in faith.

I thank thee, God, for the dreams which have moved men to hear thee and seek thee. Let their dreams move me to listen, to seek, and to find thee. For Jesus' sake. Amen.

Week 31——Day 2   **Read Phil. 1:3; Luke 17:11-19**

There are disciplines of thanksgiving. Not the least is the necessity of remembering those to whom we owe gratitude, and when we have recalled who they are, telling them of our thanks. "I thank my God in all my remembrance of you." So wrote Paul to the friends in Philippi. Surely there is someone to whom you are grateful, from whom you received a blessing but to whom you have not expressed adequate gratitude. Surprise him with a note to show you have not forgotten. Not only is it a good thing to give thanks, but, too, such a word of appreciation might be just the encouragement he needed. Both you and he may need it today.

Discipline my mind today, O God, to recall the persons to whom I owe a thanksgiving. Then direct my feelings to expression. In the Spirit of Christ. Amen.

Week 31——Day 3   Read I Chr. 16:8-34

This is one of the greatest psalms of thanksgiving in all scripture. Out of verse 29 comes one of the imperative disciplines of gratitude: *Make a gift for your gratitude.* Some cause needs more help than is likely to come, some person is having a hard time and does not know if he will get through—in gratitude for all that has been given you, will you make some gift today that will add support where a person is weak, bring cheer where someone is sad, offer hope to a soul discouraged, give resource to those waging war on sin or disease?

Discipline my heart today to sacrifice for thee, my Father, and help me to choose wisely what offering to make. For Christ's sake. Amen.

Week 31——Day 4   Read I Cor. 13:9-13

Leonard Ecker, a Michigan schoolteacher, underwent a corneal transplant. At thirty-four he could see for the first time—not clearly yet, but as in a mirror dimly still. "I'm still more familiar with my old world," he said in the first days of vague sight. "I'm not as sure of myself in getting around as I was before. But my world is full of nothing but hope." Ecker was

145

living through a true parable for us all. It is easier to live the old life, to be satisfied with former ways. It is painful to see the light of God in Christ. We cannot yet make out the truth clearly. We stumble. But there is hope because we know the love of God. Thanks be to him for that.

We hope, our Father, because we have faith. We have faith because thou hast loved us in Christ Jesus. We pray in his Spirit. Amen.

Week 31——Day 5 Read Ps. 16:5-6

Rufus Jones reflected thus on the home in which he grew up:

I am most of all thankful for my birthplace and early nurture in the warm atmosphere of a spiritually minded home. I can never be grateful enough for what was done for me by my progenitors before I came on the scene. They produced the spiritual atmosphere of my youth. I became heir of a vast invisible inheritance, more important in my life than ancestral lands or chests full of the gold of Ophir. There is nothing I would exchange for that.

What would it mean if our descendants could look back with the same gratitude to us—for what we did to create the atmosphere of faith and love which makes their lives rich?

O God, as we are faithful to our ancestors in gratitude, may we also be true to our descendants in trust. For Christ's sake. Amen.

In 1851, as the country faced the threat of disunion, Daniel Webster invoked the memory of George Washington by quoting a bit of Roman oratory: "I wish these things: one, that in dying I may leave a free people; nothing greater than this can be given me by the immortal God; the second, that each man may prove worthy of the republic." Webster's instinct was probably true in ascribing these sentiments to Washington. Surely no line in Washington's character was stronger than the sense of duty, of what he owed to the commonwealth of Virginia and later the unified nation of states. It would be a sad day for any man's character to allow such a sense of duty to the public good to wither away. May God grant that we prove worthy of the labor expended and the price paid by the republic for our blessings.

O God, may we never cease to give thanks that others have labored and we have entered into their labors. Even Jesus Christ our Lord. Amen.

What did Peter mean, "cleansed their hearts by faith"? It would be wonderful if we could ask him, but that is not necessary. We can ask the man who was sick with guilt over wrong he had done and then found that he could believe God still loved him. We can ask the woman who was afraid of death and then found that she could trust God to be the Lord of both life and death. We could ask anyone whose hardness of heart had been broken by following Christ's way of compassion. So it is that trusting both life and death to God, sin and fear and hardness of heart are purged away.

*Save us, our Father, through the grace of the Lord Jesus
doing the same for us. In his name. Amen.*

WEEK 32

You are Simon . . . ? You shall be called [Peter].—John 1:42

When Simon Becomes Peter

Week 32——Day 1   Read I John 3:1-3

In the meditations of this week we shall be thinking of the
process and transformation by which Simon becomes Peter.
Seven incidents from the life of Simon Peter will reveal to us
the stages and experiences through which every person must
pass, as did Peter, in his attainment unto the full life in Christ.

In does not yet appear what we shall be, but by his power
God can make each of us who is Simon into Peter, the rock.
This is the promise. God can do what he promises if we will
have it so. Read again the account of Jesus' first meeting with
Simon in John 1:35-42. We start with that hope. *I am Simon.
I shall be Peter.*

*O God, however unpromising our prospects, give us confi-
dence that thou canst make us rocks of strength and faith.
For Jesus' sake. Amen.*

This is the way a great loyalty begins; we have a call to a better life, a better way, and we say, "Yes." The thing is to be ready, open to hearing the call when it comes. Often we don't see or hear when God's call comes, and the opportunity passes us by. As Stephen Benét put it, the vision is often "too hard, too strange, too new, too unbelievable, too difficult, warring too much with common easy ways." So it must have seemed to Simon Peter when Jesus first said, "Follow me." But Peter went. It was his greatest chance, and he did not miss it, Moreover, he was not so entangled with possessions and connections that he could not break free to respond to the call when it came.

O God, in the impulses to follow an inspiration, or in brief encounters with goodness, beauty, or human need, may we hear thy call to follow. Let us be free enough to answer. In Jesus' name. Amen.

Weeks or months later Peter made this great confession— the most decisive any person can make about Christ. He didn't know all the answers; he wasn't sure of the outcome; but he knew Jesus. He was ready to stake his life on that. So it is with all of us—we have to act, to declare our faith even when the end is not known. *Especially* when the end is not known. Whatever Peter may have believed or doubted, perceived or misunderstood about Jesus at this time, he made the great commitment and confession *by which he later became sure.*

Our Father, we do not ask to see the distant scene. Give us faith to confess Christ as Lord and go with him in all confidence. In his name we pray. Amen.

Week 32——Day 4   Read Mark 14:66-72

Peter was afraid. In his fear he failed his Master, even as we fail him, too. Furthermore, this was *after* Jesus told him, "You are Peter, and on this rock I will build my church."

What a comfort that this story is here! Only Peter would have confessed it of himself, how he failed his Lord. Peter was human. This man who was the rock failed! Yet with the likes of Peter Christ builds his kingdom. Thank God that he does, or what would we do; what hope would we have?

O God, may we be honest to acknowledge how we have failed thee in fear, and by denial of Christ. With thee there is forgiveness. Through Jesus Christ. Amen.

Week 32——Day 5   Read John 21:4-8, 15-19

Jesus came to Peter in his failure and forgave him. Christ does come to us in our failures and restore us. The past is past, over and done. Now we begin again. "Feed my sheep," says Jesus Christ. Take up my task.

We have to face our failures, not avoid them, deny them, rationalize them. We face them under the forgiving eyes of Christ. Then in humility we accept his forgiveness and take up his task.

In the joy of thy forgiveness, our Father, may we take up the task which Christ offers, to do his will. For his name's sake. Amen.

It was not easy for Peter to do these things. It was hard for Simon the Jew to become Peter the Christian. There came times when Peter wavered with his strange new call and task, but he kept coming back to it, even though it meant crossing dangerous frontiers, moving into unfamiliar ways, losing favor with men, and doing things that meant shame.

The Christian task always demands the difficult duty—forgiveness of those we hate, acceptance of those we despise, kindness to the ungrateful, honor to the outcast and lowly. The Simon in us who would refuse must become Peter who accepts.

O God, we know that thy will calls us to do difficult things. By thy sustaining power uphold us to do them. In Jesus' name. Amen.

The last scene in this life journey is hidden from our eyes. Today's verse of scripture may be a hint of it. We do not know what happened to the Christians to whom Peter belonged in Rome under Nero in A.D. 64. They were martyred—tortured and put to death for sport. Peter could hardly have escaped. By constant devotion to God, the steady serving of Christ, the continuous companionship of the risen Lord, Peter came to his crown of life—fearless preaching in Rome, then to lay down his life.

You are Simon, you shall be Peter. Christ says it to you with power to make it come true.

O God, in the hour of trial may we not waver but in rock-like faith follow in the train of the faithful. For Christ's sake. Amen.

WEEK 33

What does the Lord require?
You shall love your neighbor.—Lev. 19:18

On the Street Where We Live

Week 33——Day 1   **Read Acts 1:6-8**

Thomas Carlyle's wife told of the time her husband set out to look for a house in London—armed with three maps of Great Britain and two of the world in his pocket. How irrelevant and ridiculous! But no more so than the use we often make of the Christian gospel. It is a gospel for the world. What we often need and sometimes do not have, however, is a street map of the neighborhood where we live, showing us what the gospel promises to and demands of the people right there. Jesus started his disciples on their mission in Jerusalem.

Turn our vision this day, our Father, toward our Christian duties on the street where we live. In Jesus' name. Amen.

Week 33——Day 2   **Read John 13:5-9**

In *Lost Men of American History* Stewart Holbrook quotes what Thomas Studley, one of the Virginia pioneers of 1607, wrote of the building of their miserable huts: "Captaine

Smith, by his own example, good words and faire promises, put some of his crew to binding thatch on the vine poles; and always did Smith bear ye greatest taske himself, neglecting a hut for Smith until all others were under cover."

Help us, our Father, to find and fill the role of servant in home, business, community, and friendship, bearing the greatest burdens ourselves for the sake of others. For Christ's sake. Amen.

Week 33——Day 3   Read Acts 5:1-11

Ananias and Sapphira are progenitors of a long line of people who have died of holding back the proceeds of their earnings from the common good and needs of all men. Not all their descendants died so dramatically, but death of the spirit surely comes to everyone who clutches and grabs for himself the resources for which his brother's need may be great. Something terrible happens to the soul of a man who holds back for his own satisfaction that which his brother must have in order to live.

If I am keeping back from my brothers' needs any proceeds of thy goodness to me, O God, release me from my fears and greed that they and I may both live. For Christ's sake. Amen.

Week 33——Day 4   Read Acts 24:22-27

Among the more contemptible men of the Bible, Felix rates a high place. The Roman historian Tacitus says of him, "with all manner of cruelty and lust he exercised the functions of a prince with the disposition of a slave." He had no principles that we can discover; yet he had great power. Disposed to serve nobody but himself, he was a slave to greed, fear, and political favors. Felix sat where many of us sit—in a position to wield great power. Felix had the disposition many of us will have unless we have surrendered to an allegiance that makes us the servant as well as the master of men.

O God, give us the disposition of the Prince of Peace and the functions of a servant of men. In Christ our Lord. Amen.

Week 33——Day 5   Read Lev. 19:15-16

In H. R. L. Sheppard's *More Shepherd's Pie* is an anecdote first told by Sir Edward Burne-Jones. A newspaper published this editorial correction: "Instead of being arrested yesterday as we stated for kicking his wife down a flight of stairs and hurling a kerosene lamp after her Revd. James P. Wellman died unmarried four years ago." Quite a difference! How many who read the original account noted the correction? How often do we repeat something we have not verified about another and so hurt someone by slander we should not have spoken?

Forbid, our Father, that by careless word we should ever stand forth against the life of our neighbor. In Christ's name. Amen.

Week 33——Day 6   Read John 4:16-19, 28-29

John Robert Clarke in his book of much wisdom, *The Importance of Being Imperfect*, observed:

What we usually want is a fancy human being with no flaws. We may love that [imaginary] picture rather than the real person behind it. We are disappointed when the person we love does not conform to our picture . . . one might suppose we would tear up the picture and start all over. On the contrary, we keep the picture and tear up the person.

At the Samaritan well Jesus sought the woman behind the picture, less admirable than the picture, yet to her he spoke some of his greatest words. In the Spirit of Christ we can seek real persons behind their false pictures and love them for all their flaws. We can at the same time, with God's help, reveal our own real selves behind the prepared pictures.

May we accept people with joy in what they really are and by our love help them to be the best they can be. For Jesus' sake. Amen.

Week 33——Day 7   Read Phil. 2:25-30

Surely Epaphroditus is numbered among your acquaintances. Who is he? He is a person who quietly undertakes a ministry to someone else at extreme risk and expense to himself. He is a person who pitches in to do the work at hand for a great purpose, whatever the work may be. He is a person who brings good news to another who is downcast. He is a person who with courage stands up to be counted for God when the battle is joined. Brother, fellow worker, fellow soldier, messenger, minister—Epaphroditus. You know him. For all such men, thank God. Honor them and follow them!

Lord, may we honor all who serve thee, especially those who, in the service of others, take their task and post out of sight and out of glory. For Christ's sake. Amen.

WEEK 34

Exciting Adventures in High Fidelity

Week 34——Day 1   **Read II Tim. 4:6-7**

A newspaper advertisement caught the eye with this banner headline: FIVE EXCITING ADVENTURES IN HIGH FIDELITY. YOURS FREE. It referred to recordings of music by Stravinsky, Copland, Moussorgsky, and Prokofiev being offered by a record club. High fidelity is an idea that belongs not exclusively to music. Paul summed up his life as one of *high fidelity:* "I have kept the faith," he told Timothy. High fidelity to the great commandments—love of God and love of neighbor—is an exciting adventure. It is not free. One must labor unceasingly to achieve it. But it is exciting to reproduce in the life of each day that which God set before us as the way of life—highest allegiance to him, uncompromising concern for the well-being of our neighbors.

God, let the music of our living this day be high fidelity to thy love for us. In Christ's spirit. Amen.

Week 34——Day 2   **Read I Cor. 2:2**

High fidelity to the cross! Paul knew nothing among the Corinthians except the crucified Savior. In other words his life faithfully echoed the almost unbelievable truths which the cross revealed—even while we were unrepentant sinners Christ died for us, and so opened the way for us to return to our

Father's seeking love; by the stripes of one who suffered there for us we are healed of our anger, pride, lust, and self-will. What a difference it would make if we would live our lives in high fidelity to the cross! By God's grace we can.

Enable us, our Father, to find our heart and soul, mind and strength, in thee. So may we be faithful to thy fidelity to us. In Jesus' name. Amen.

Week 34——Day 3   **Read Acts 20:28-31; Eph. 4:29**

High fidelity to the Church! Paul admonished the people of Ephesus to be faithful in feeding the Church of the Lord. How may we feed the Church? Eduard Thurneysen, a German pastor, suggests one important way—through pastoral conversation among the members. "Our speech must be measured by the question of whether it can exist before the Word of God." He referred to edifying talk with each other by those who have heard the Word of God. He went on to say, "[Our speech] either is useless, unfruitful, evil talk which gives nothing to him who hears it—talk out of which nothing grows and develops—or it is that talk which imparts grace to him who hears it."

Lord, speak to us that we may speak in faithful echoes of thy word. For Christ's sake. Amen.

Week 34——Day 4   **Read I Cor. 6:19**

High fidelity to the faithful of the past! How much more exciting life would be if we could reproduce in our lives even a little of the faithfulness once given to us by which we have been brought to this day. Some loved us beyond all our deserving. Some paid with their lives for our protection from danger. Some encouraged us when we gave scant promise. Some denied themselves that we might have life in abundance. What faithfulness is required (and from how many) that we can even be where we are today!

O God, we would render in high fidelity our debt to all who paid some price for our privilege. In Jesus' name. Amen.

Week 34——Day 5 Read Ps. 145:4

High fidelity to the future! Isn't it hard to be faithful to the future? He who builds a house well for the sake of those who will live in it when the builder is gone is faithful to the future. He who in a manner most fitting lauds the works of God to his children and their children is faithful to the future. Few men possess any adequate faith or spiritual resource for the living of these days that someone before him has not given him in a sense of high fidelity to a future he could not see.

O God, forbid that any shall stumble in the days to come, because we fail our high fidelity to them now. For Christ's sake. Amen.

Week 34——Day 6 Read I Pet. 2:9-10

Alas, so many of us put this wonderful experience in reverse: "Once we were God's people, but now we are no people." The quickening spirit all exhausted within us, the glorious inheritance of faith faded away, we are hardly alive to God anymore. This happens so often to a church. Driving through lovely

Duchess County in New York my heart was lifted by the distant sight of a beautiful white church spire. Upon reaching the building I discovered it had become an antique shop! How many churches have likewise dwindled to "antique shops" in all but name, because people have not been faithful to what they were called to be—God's people.

By the life of faithful prayer may we keep our church not as a museum of memories but as a fountain of life. For Jesus' sake. Amen.

Week 34——Day 7   **Read Mark 8:34**

Said Polonius to his son in Shakespeare's *Hamlet:*

> This above all: to thine own self be true,
> And it must follow, as the night the day,
> Thou canst not then be false to any man.

In one sense, yes, but true to which self? We have many selves; "legion" is our name. Only when one is faithful to a high and commanding cause or love beyond self can he hope not to be false to others. There is no such thing as being true to a self that is not in turn true to something greater than self. We need the love of Christ in order not to serve our lesser selves.

"Make me a captive, Lord, and then I shall be free"—free of selfish ambition and so at liberty to love thee. For Jesus' sake. Amen.

Be reconciled to your brother.—Matt. 5:24

Walls or Bridges?

Week 35——Day 1   **Read Rom. 12:14-17**

In his address in Oslo after he had received the Nobel Prize for Peace in 1958 Father Dominique Pire said, "Men build too many walls and not enough bridges." How easy it is to build walls. People whose problems and needs we do not share we shut out from our concern—up goes a wall. Between ourselves and people with whose faith or ideas we disagree we build walls of antagonism and contention. Against one who has slighted or wronged us we bear grudge and resentment—the stones of a massive wall. Forebearance, reconciliation, understanding, and acceptance—these are bridges which unite us in the bond of humanity.

So far as it depends on us, our Father, let us build bridges of reconciliation to all those from whom we stand divided. For Christ's sake. Amen.

Week 35——Day 2   **Read Luke 23:32-34**

Jesus' first word from the cross was a last word of love in the face of sin. It gave never-to-be-forgotten demonstration that where a person can confront sin with love he opens the way for new life. Homes have been saved because parents spoke a last word of forgiveness to children, or children to parents. What of husband or wife who kept the initiative of love against sin's blight? Who could number the personal relationships which have been saved by the forgiveness of one partner who took all the hostility of the other into himself and turned it back in love? The cross has few greater things to teach us than that we must bear the sins and hurts of others if we are to help God heal the hardness of heart that is between us, and between men and God.

Father, forgive them, and us, for none of us knows what he does. In the spirit of him who forgave us. Amen.

Week 35——Day 3   Read I Cor. 13:4-6

The *New English Bible* translates verse six, "Love keeps no score of wrongs." What a wonderful way to put it! Is it not judgment against what we commonly do? A writer tells that in Polynesia, where the natives spend much of their time in fighting, it is customary for each man to keep some reminders of his hatred. They suspend articles from the roofs of their huts to keep alive memory of wrongs done to them. Perhaps we are more subtle about it, but do we not keep suspended in our minds the memories of how people offended us, took some advantage of us, or in some way did us in? Christian love, on the contrary, keeps no such score. Such love is eager to be reconciled with every "offender."

Our Father, teach us how to forget wrongs by rejoicing in the right. Allow us not to make light of evil but to overcome evil with good. In Jesus' name. Amen.

At the entrance of the new Coventry Cathedral is an International Youth Center. It was built by German youth who labored without salary for six months as an effort toward reconciliation. What these young people did to be reconciled to those who had been their enemies is demonstration of the Christian way wherever enmity has come between people. We are entrusted with the message of reconciliation. We must show it in every way humanly possible to those whom we have hurt.

Thou has dismissed our trespasses against thee, our Father; so let us not reckon the wrongs of others against us. For Jesus' sake. Amen.

What a pitiable state Lazarus was in! Poor, diseased, hungry, set upon by dogs—he must have been seen at the gate by the rich man. He recognized Lazarus in the nether world. Here in this world, gorgeously apparelled and feasting sumptuously, he felt no anguish for the miserable fellow at his gate. He postponed his anguish until later—much later! As God permits us all to do. We can put off our anguish for our fellow creatures. But all the imagery of this parable is saying that something frightful happens to a man who feels no anguish over human suffering. We were made to be reconciled with our brothers, even the poor brother at the distant gate. To remain unreconciled is to destroy ourselves.

Lord, fill us with anguish now over all who suffer and are in need, and let us be reconciled. For Christ's sake. Amen.

In the East Harlem Protestant Parish of New York members are encouraged in what is called "gossiping the gospel," speaking of the good news in the ordinary conversation of every day. We frequently act as if the gospel were "classified information." Notice that in the book of Acts Christians gossiped the gospel whenever they had the chance. "We cannot but speak of what we have seen and heard." It was their speaking that made the difference! Because of what they said people knew the source of the power for what was done through them. The very act of gossiping the gospel reconciled them to all those to whom they told the good news of what God had done. One can hardly tell another person the wonderful news of God's love and still be an enmity with him. To believe in God's love is to speak of it, and to speak of it is to make it real. And when it is real we practice it.

Lord, let me speak this day for thee, that my brother and I may share thy gracious gifts. In the spirit of Christ. Amen.

There is an old story of two Irishmen who agreed to fight until such time as one or the other cried, "Enough!" On went the battle for over an hour. At last one faintly gasped the magic word. The other, in exhausted relief blurted, "Egad! I have been trying to think of that word for the last half hour!" Many times we carry chips on our shoulders or bear grudges toward another when we should cry, "Enough!" Is there another person with whom you could be reconciled this day, saying, in effect, enough of old animosity?

Let it be enough of continuing ill will toward one whom we blame in our hearts. By thy grace we would be reconciled, our Father. In Jesus' name. Amen.

WEEK 36

We are members one of another.—Eph. 4:25

Never Disconnected

Week 36——Day 1   **Read I Cor. 12:25-26**

From an unexpected source comes a wonderful description of what a Christian family should be and do. In the musical play and motion picture *West Side Story* one boy sings of what it means to belong to the Jets, a neighborhood gang on New York City's West Side. When you belong to the Jets "you're never disconnected, you always walk by two's, by three's, by fours." How better could you say what it ought to mean being in a Christian home, or church, or community? Never alone but always connected to others! Never a lonely picket, but always walking in company!

Our Father, are there any in our family, on our street, even in our church who are "disconnected"? Let me join them to walk by two's in the strength of Christ. For his sake. Amen.

L. E. Nelson wrote these lines called "My Pompous Friend":

> His sense of dignity is strong.
> To see him stroll is fun.
> He walks as if he were a long
> Processional of one.

Many people go through life as a processional of one—forgetting that we all belong to one God and therefore belong to each other. We cannot find God or the good life all alone. We must walk in a great company. Edwin Arlington Robinson has observed that "the man who goes too far alone goes mad—in one way or another." We become real persons only through mutually affirming our membership with other people in the human family.

May we fall in step with all others who also seek thy face, O God. In Christ's name. Amen.

Burris Jenkins told of an experience which occurred in the pioneer days of the West. When a lone sheep failed to return to the fold one night the shepherds searched until they found it at the far end of the pasture. It could not be driven home and it was too heavy to carry. Finally one shepherd returned to the fold and brought the whole flock down to the lost sheep. The stray meekly followed the flock home. A wonderful picture of a church—the whole flock going out to bring one member home, all bearing the burdens of each one.

Join us in such communion with our fellow members in the church and in our homes, that the needs of each one become the cares of all, our Father. For Jesus' sake. Amen.

Week 36——Day 4   Read Acts 4:32-37

The kind of Christian communism which we see here should in no way be considered an economic pattern for us to follow. It is likewise worlds away from twentieth-century Communist totalitarianism. But well might we act as "sons of encouragement," as did the people of the apostolic pentecostal church, putting ourselves and all that we have under the constraint of the common need of our brothers. If by some resource I could encourage another person, by some skill help him in a difficult place, by some interest lift up his fallen spirit, by some gift ease the pressure of heavy demands—I know this is the offering Christ asks.

As I have been encouraged by others, so may I be a support to any whose needs appeal to my strength. For Christ's sake. Amen.

Week 36——Day 5   Read Lev. 19:17-18

From Clement of Alexandria comes the tradition that Matthew said: "If the neighbor of an elect man sin, the elect man has sinned. For had he conducted himself as the Word prescribes, his neighbor also would have been filled with such reverence for the life he has led as not to sin." It may be doubted that this sounds like Matthew; one might question the truth of his statement as it applies to all cases. Nevertheless, we do live in communities, bound together in one bundle of life. My neighbor's sins can often be traced to my weakness. I am responsible to love him in such a way that in nothing which is within my control do I give him cause for stumbling.

Fill us with concern that we give no person cause to fall in the Way, O God. In Jesus' name. Amen.

Week 36— Day 6   Read II Cor. 13:13

Paul said to the Corinthians, "All the dedicated people of God [in Ephesus?] greet you." Such was the meaning of "saints." It can have a larger meaning to us—all the *saints* in the *whole* church, past and present, greet us. Alfred N. Whitehead said, "The present is holy ground. . . . The communion of saints is a great and inspiring assemblage, but it has only one possible hall of meeting, and that is, the present." Those who have gone before and those who will come after are both part of this present moment. At the meeting place of two eternities it is good to be surrounded by "God's people" who have gone before us and who will come after. They help us to be our best.

We are surrounded by so great a company in Jesus Christ. Amen.

Week 36——Day 7   Read Matt. 7:16-21

An exciting phrase has come into use with the development of nuclear power plants. When the process of atomic fission reaches a certain stage energy begins to be generated that can be turned into power. At this point they say that the reactor has "gone critical." We might well use this phrase with reference to a family, to the church, to any other Christian group.

167

When the fission of fellowship and gospel, people and mission, reaches a certain stage in this "reactor" so that energy opens up concern for life outside the family or church, then the group has "gone critical." How about your family—your church? Have they "gone critical"?

Help us, Lord, to be moved by our beliefs, so that our actions will make a critical difference where we live. For Christ's sake. Amen.

WEEK 37

The fruit of the spirit is . . . faithfulness.—Gal. 5:22

Mind Well the Minute Particulars

Week 37——Day 1   **Read Matt. 25:23**

If we are faithful over a little God accordingly judges us as able to be faithful over much. The poet William Blake once warned, "Mind well the minute particulars." Speaking of this Alexander Miller rightly perceived, "It is not possible to serve Christ in the large and neglect the details."

What is the minute particular I ought to forgive? How about the minute particular of kindness that it is in my power to do today? What minute particular of faithful discipline do I neglect?

Test our faithfulness this day, O God, by putting us to the possible task while we trust the large design to thee, enabling

*us by thy Holy Spirit whose gift is faithfulness. In Jesus' name.
Amen.*

Week 37——Day 2   Read Isa. 26:1-4

Serious speculation has been made that future space ships may
go off upon voyages that will last for generations. The way,
whether by arresting the aging process, suspending animation,
or allowing generations to be born and to pass away on the voyage, is not now known. Were such a trip to become a possibility what would you take with you—what disciplines would you
demand of yourself in order that the heritage of your mind and
faith be not lost? In the deepest sense this is not speculation.
We are on such a voyage through space. What great treasures
of faith are you keeping for those who come after?

*Let us stay our minds on thee, O God, that those who follow
us may strengthen the faith of generations to come. In Christ
we pray. Amen.*

Week 37——Day 3   Read 1 Tim. 1:12

The gift of the spirit is faithfulness. This New Testament
writer gave us further word as to what that means. "He judged
me faithful by appointing me to his service." It is as though
the writer were saying that faithfulness must be the mark of
one who serves Christ—that would mean faithfulness to all
others bound together with us in the bundle of life.

Imagine that we are climbing a mountain peak together. I
must belay the rope where I stand, or others will be in danger.
For my family, I hold the rope to which they cling for life.

169

For my community, I can weaken the position of the whole common life by unfaithfully letting go the rope of integrity, of righteousness, of concern. For those in my employ, under my supervision, in my care, I may hold the rope of their lives. I must be faithful with the rope where I hold it; this is the service to which I am appointed. I need the gift of the Spirit.

Others depend on me this day. For their sakes, O God, I would be true. In the Spirit of Christ. Amen.

Week 37——Day 4   **Read I Sam. 20:42**

This verse concludes a long account of the friendship between David and Jonathan. The whole chapter is a wonderful account of loyalty.

Some years ago Dean Christian Gauss of Princeton asked members of the faculty, "What are the six most important words in the English language?" "Loyalty" headed the list; then followed *courage, sportsmanship, sanity, self-respect, humor, truth, yes, no, knowledge.* An interesting vocabulary, in many ways a strange list. Notably lacking are the great nouns and verbs, God, faith, love. Surely "loyalty" belongs near the top of that list. It would be a sad reckoning up of any life for which loyalty would not come to mind as a fitting summary.

To friendship, to trusts, to thee, O God, by thy Spirit keep me faithful. In Jesus' name. Amen.

"This night your soul is required of you." The words sound like the crack of doom—which they may be. We usually associate those words with the final judgment of death. But a man's soul may be required of him more than once in his life. My soul may be required of me tonight in a moral choice I must make, in an adversity I must bear, in a witness I must give for Christ. What if my soul has been lost to barns, goods, and possessions? It has happened that men have been unequal to the demands of an hour because their barns were in the way.

I pray, God, that by thy grace with the gift of faithfulness, my soul may be equal to every requirement. For Christ's sake. Amen.

Of what interest to us now are all these names since even Luke admits the genealogy is not really historical but only "supposed" to be the family lineage? The genealogy identifies the life of Jesus not only with one nation (Abraham), but with all mankind (Adam, the son of God). It symbolizes further the long painful process by which God prepares his way. How many obscure people he used for his purpose! I am grateful that Joanan and Melchi and the other 73 could be used by God, that they were faithful though they could not see the final issue of their faithfulness. I also trust that God can use me in the way of preparation for some distant purpose.

O God, help me to be faithful to the past and to the future, that the promises may not, on my account, be vain for anyone. In Jesus' name. Amen.

"I will give you your life." This God promises to do no matter where we may go, whether around the corner or to the ends of the earth. More than breathing and consciousness, my life is my soul held in faithfulness to God, integrity of character because I love God. We need never be afraid of where life will send us—God will go with us, will be there when we arrive. In every place, if we fight the battle that is asked of us, for which ordeal God gives his Spirit, if we do not needlessly mourn the past nor cross all the future bridges of imagination, he will give us our life, our souls, our integrity.

Though life take all else from me, O God, give me my soul in the gift of thy Spirit. In the Spirit of Christ. Amen.

WEEK 38

The fruit of the Spirit is . . . self-control.—Gal. 5:22-23

Head Over Heels

"He's head over heels," we sometimes say of a person in love or in debt. It means completely "gone." Literally head over heels is a fine way to stand in all the great moments of life— our heads in command of our heels. Tragedy follows where a person turns "heels over head"—in some moment of truth running from the best that he knows, heels over head; carelessly trampling the feelings and rights of others, heels over head. Paul said to the Corinthians, "Keep head over heels," that is to say, "Be watchful, stand firm." Let your feet never be planted with the grinding boot of tyranny, but only upon the steps of love.

O God, we would be head over heels in faithful love toward thee, through the Spirit's grace of self-control. In Jesus' name. Amen.

Week 38——Day 2   Read Eccl. 5:1 2

It has been said of Honoré de Balzac, great French novelist, that "he was a man who always had more to say than he said." A fine tribute this would be for any person. How insufferable that we should inflict on our friends *all* that we might have to say! What poor taste; yea, how unkind in many instances to say *all* that we know! We cannot learn if we do not listen. Many people will not listen because they will not, or cannot, stop talking. The writer of Ecclesiastes put it well: "To draw near to listen is better than to offer the sacrifice of fools." Much talk, without discipline of self-control, is the sacrifice most fools offer.

Help us to guard our lips this day, O God. Let us listen to those who want and need to talk to us. For Jesus' sake. Amen.

Week 38——Day 3   Read Ps. 101:1-4

Edwin Way Teale tells in his *North With the Spring* of a small species of singing birds whose eyes outweigh their brains.

It is a disproportion that frequently afflicts the human species as well. Many people have allowed their eyes to outweigh their brains, indiscriminately gorging their eyes from morning till night with unevaluated sights and spectacles, with no judgment rendered by the brain. Our minds quickly fill with the cheap and tawdry. Moral responsibility insists upon full sight of the worst. It will not tolerate promiscuous, pointless, and prodigal waste of sight upon that which is base.

Let the mind which was in Christ be in us also, our Father, to teach us the meaning of what we see. For his sake. Amen.

Week 38——Day 4　　　　Read Acts 7:21; Matt. 13:52

Luke's description of the Athenians comes also as an indictment of ourselves. We are caught up in a never ending pursuit of novelty, eager to follow any pied piper of fashion or fad. Advertising apparently succeeds on the premise that if a thing has a *new* ingredient, we will rush to get it. Count the appearances of the word *new* in the TV commercials. Grateful we are for much that is new and good; let us also be attentive to the householder of whom Jesus spoke who brings out of his treasure both what is new and old—old habits of integrity, old moral standards, old loyalties of faith. Against the engulfing tides of novelty we need the grace of self-control.

Lord, let us neither fear the new, nor discard the old, until we judge them both by Christ. In his name. Amen.

The *New English Bible* translates verse 34: "As he could not get at the truth because of the hubbub he ordered him to be taken into barracks." All praise to that commandant for his firm self-control; he is in the noble company of those who have honored truth above uproar. He wasn't swept away by the violence of mass hysteria. He insisted on knowing who Paul was and exactly what he had done. Indeed his assumption that Paul was an Egyptian terrorist turned out to be mistaken, as assumptions born of uproar frequently do. The man's name was Claudius Lysias. We could make him the patron saint of all public and private uproars, the saint who would say to us, "Let us have the truth instead of clamor!"

Grant, Lord, that we may never yield to hubbubs of feeling, but by the grace of thy Spirit may seek the truth in all the conflicts of life. For Christ's sake. Amen.

The lovely story of Ruth has been instructive and encouraging to faithful readers for nearly 2,500 years. There is so much here for both heart and mind: Ruth's lovely act of devotion to Naomi, the unselfish and "international" spirit of Boaz, the strong sense of family solidarity, the symbolism that Jesus is descended from a man of Israel and a woman of Moab. We must not overlook one of the subordinate points of the story— the fine reticence and reserve of Boaz toward Ruth, a seeking after honor, the concern for understanding in the community which was so important to this man and woman. Things are done differently today than they were then, but their behavior has lessons for us who would put off the garments of honor and social concern. No family ever can live entirely unto itself. Families all around us are bound in communities, which we help to make for good or ill by our behavior. We need the fruit of the spirit, self-control, for their sakes as well as our own.

O Lord, let us never in any way be the cause over which others may stumble to their hurt or dishonor. Rather let us help in the name of him in whom we are bound in one bundle of life. For Jesus' sake. Amen.

Week 38——Day 7   **Read Prov. 27:1**

America discovered a new expression on the day Col. John Glenn made his orbital flight. "All systems are go!"—meaning, "everything is in perfect order, ready for launch, or ready for the next stage." One of the amazing facts about Glenn's capsule, *Friendship 7*, was that every system of control or safety was backed up by a supporting system. Failure or emergency at any place could be met by a ready system instantly available. It suggests the question, Are all systems *go* for the day of emergency that may come to us—systems of faith, forgiveness, fidelity to the highest?

Life counts us down to some day of reckoning, our Father. May each day find us more ready to meet it because we have been faithful with all the capacity thou hast given us. In Jesus' name. Amen.

I will trust, and not be afraid.—Isa. 12:2

I Don't Understand All I Know

Week 39——Day 1   **Read John 9:25**

An old ship carpenter in New England once said, concerning a difficult piece of construction: "I know that can be done." When asked how he knew he replied, "Don't ask me so many questions; I can't understand all I know." How true of us all. We act every day upon truth that we know but cannot "understand." This is particularly so in matters of faith. Said Jeremy Taylor of Christian belief in the incarnation and the immortality of the soul, "We are often sure of the thing, when we are not sure of the argument."

It is as important to understand as much of Christian truth as possible. Beyond that it is necessary to live by what we *know* —that God is love and that God was in Christ.

Help us, O God, to live by the trusting affection of our hearts when they are stayed on thee. In Jesus' name. Amen.

Week 39——Day 2   **Read Acts 12:12-17**

"But Peter continued knocking." The words have a special meaning for multitudes of Christians of whom the same thing can be said: *They continue knocking.* Doorways into reconciliation with others from whom they have been estranged do not open, *they continue knocking in love.* Doorways leading out of doubt into confidence do not open, but *they continue knocking in search.* Doorways leading out of loneliness and despair into gladness and hope do not open, but *they continue knocking in faithfulness.* Doorways into the assurance of God's presence do not open, but *they continue knocking in prayer.*

Let all those who persist in knocking at the doorways of life know that thine angels are with them, our Father. In Jesus' name. Amen.

Week 39——Day 3 Read Matt. 7:21

The Spanish philosopher Jose Ortega y Gasset once said: "I do not recall that any civilization ever perished from an attack of doubt . . . Civilizations usually die through the ossification of their traditional faith, through an arteriosclerosis of their beliefs." How well put for our own sober thought. We should not fear our doubts; doubt is the other side of the coin of faith. What we ought to fear is the arteriosclerosis of belief; that is, the hardening of the channels through which the life blood of Christian living flows out to men in their need.

O God, even when we cannot always say, Lord, Lord, with conviction about all things, let us do those things which Christ commands. In them may our common life live. For his sake. Amen.

Week 39——Day 4 Read Exod. 14:21-29

An old Jewish legend recounted by Victor Gollancz has it that "when Moses threw the wand into the Red Sea, quite contrary to the expected miracle, the sea did not divide itself to leave a dry passage for the Jews. Not until the first man had jumped into the sea did the promised miracle happen and the waves recede." One gains little from dispute over how things happened in legends. But truth is here. Seas of difficulty and hindrance, whether in ourselves or in the world, do not roll back before magic wands. They are moved when men jump into them with faith in the power and promises of God.

We would not depend on any magic or trick, our Father, to move through trouble, but upon thy power to sustain us in the deep waters. Through Jesus Christ our Lord. Amen.

Week 39——Day 5   Read Exod. 15:2

Among the reinforcements of my faith is the awareness that my God is he who was also my father's God, and my father's father worshiped God before us. In our love of the same God, and in his love toward us, the generations find common dwelling. Doubts may hinder faith; perplexity may baffle understanding; yet this we know: Our fathers in their pilgrimage trusted God. He was to them a cloud by day and a fire by night. They were neither confounded nor ashamed.

There is deep satisfaction in walking where they walked. Because God was their God, we believe more surely he is our God, and we exalt him with joy.

May our children also exult in thee, O Lord, because thou art our God. In Jesus' name. Amen.

Week 39——Day 6   Read Mark 8:35

There is buried in a Jerusalem cemetery a whole company of soldiers from Australia who died fighting with Allenby in

1917. One of these men was a Jew. On his grave you may read his name, followed by this inscription: "He died far from his homeland, but near to his country." Leave aside the consideration of Zionism, which is questionable; it is a word to ponder whenever we think of our gospel. He who is faithful to Christ must often die far from the homeland of his hopes, but near to the country of his God. Sometimes it will have to be death of the body. At other times the death of former and familiar life and hopes. But he who must so die for Christ finds life in the country of God.

May we be willing so to die to former things of self that we may gain the country of thy will. Through Jesus Christ our Lord. Amen.

Week 39——Day 7 Read Acts 9:36-43

It is certain that many of us have never known anyone by the name of Tabitha or Dorcas. It is also certain that most of us could name at least one person whom this passage perfectly describes, full of good works and acts of charity. At the death of such people who has not wished for a Peter to come and say, "Arise"? Tabithas always die too young. Perhaps we wish for the wrong miracle. By telling of these events Luke bears witness to a resurrection power. Surely we are not to suppose it was a power for only a fortunate few such as Aeneas and Tabitha. It is for everyone. Therefore we will trust and not be afraid.

Lord, increase our faith till we hear thee say to some Tabitha whom we have loved, "Arise!" In Jesus' name. Amen.

My father is working still.—John 5:1⁷

Caution: God at Work

Week 40——Day 1   Read Ps. 46:8-9; John 5:17

Driving along the highway one frequently sees signs: *Caution: Men at Work.* If we used imagination as we journeyed through life we would become aware of many situations where a sign ought to read: *Caution: God at Work.* God is at work in the promptings of conscience which warn us to beware of destructive things we are tempted to do, in the working of love and forgiveness to heal broken relationships between people, in the reaping of ill will and social deterioration that comes from seeds of injustice and discrimination. God is at work among us everywhere. We need to take caution.

Open our eyes, our Father, to see thee when thou art working thy will toward us this day. In Jesus' name. Amen.

Week 40——Day 2   Read Acts 16:25-34

William E. Hocking once wrote of the elusive power men have of taking fire under the influence of strong leaders: "any man's worth may be multiplied tenfold under the magic of great leadership. But no investigation of the solitary human being under the highly uninspiring environment of the testing room could detect the degree of his kindling capacity."

What do you imagine your "kindling capacity" to be? Have you kept your spirit sensitive to inspiration and the appeal of holiness, so that when the Holy Spirit comes near you catch fire with power?

Kindle us, O God, that our worth for Christ may be multiplied tenfold. For his sake we pray. Amen.

Week 40——Day 3　　　Read Acts 15:22-29; Luke 11:13

A most remarkable statement for the Jerusalem church to send down to Antioch, "It has seemed good to the Holy Spirit and to us. . . ." The church was so conscious of being guided by the Spirit of God that it could be said in all confidence that this seems good to the Holy Spirit.

Alas, what has sometimes *seemed* good to the Spirit has later turned out to be good only for the devil. Nevertheless, when a church finds itself moved to new service or to greater zeal for righteousness there comes a sureness that the Holy Spirit is present and pleased. Jesus promised that the Father will give the Holy Spirit to those who ask him. We test all spirits by the Spirit of Christ; the Holy Spirit we know by the fruits of righteousness which he brings.

As thou hast promised, O God, through prophet and Christ, pour out thy renewing Spirit upon the church. Through Jesus Christ our Lord. Amen.

These words from Ivor Brown:

Comfort is one of the admirable words which have turned soft and it needs to be re-stiffened to its proper shape and value. It is, by origin, the giver of strength and valor. But the ubiquitous advertisement of "All Modern Comforts" hints mainly at central heating and other niceties of plumbing.

One is not depreciating the pleasures and utility of these in wishing more substance and dignity for the grand old word. This has become so dwarfed and so insipid that the unlettered Christian of today may easily think of the Holy Ghost, the Comforter, as a rather sickly source of sentimental consolation, a celestial crooner, almost, instead of an ally in the good fight and bringer of mettle and resolve.

Come, Holy Comforter, and gird us for the fight that we may be able to stand in the evil day, and having done all, to stand. For Christ's sake. Amen.

"God has made everything beautiful in its time." Louise Townsend Nicholl has put the affirmation in a poem, "How Beautiful It Is!" Her thought is that beauty has nothing to say to the brokenhearted, yet it can lead the eyes away, "and while they linger the quivering heart will stay." "Anaesthetic for too great an ill," she calls it. This is beauty's great benediction, to lead the eyes and mind away—not to forget or avoid sorrow's pain, but by counterbalance of the beauty of what God has made to lift the soul from sorrow's depths.

Our Father, let the solace of beauty put the thought of eternity into our minds. In Jesus' name. Amen.

Week 40——Day 6   Read Acts 2:1-13

Peter's sermon following the outpouring of the Holy Spirit lifts this chapter to towering heights in all the ranges of scripture. One almost incidental detail serves well as subject for reflection. Couple verse 13 with Luke 23:36. There were mockers at the crucifixion and mockers at Pentecost. Apparently some will always mock no matter what is done by God or man. It frightens you, doesn't it, that God's actions are never so clear that we will automatically be impressed? I wonder how often we have all mocked at some revelation and didn't know it. Mocking is a poor business.

Touch our vision with faith and our understanding with imagination that we may not mock thee in any but praise thee in all thy works. In Jesus' name. Amen.

Week 40——Day 7   Read I John 4:13-16

Winter is the season of promise, even while it is a time of sleep and death. From winter's commencement the days begin to grow longer, the sun to rise higher in the heavens. In the winter of our soul's life, whether it be in sleep, in coldness of heart, or in death, God gives promise and sign that rebirth and waking are ahead. Winter buds carry promise of foliage and fruit to come. God is at work in many invisible ways initiating the new life of the seasons ahead.

God and man together have added greater sacrament to

nature's winter. God's gift of his Son redeems winter, and all the seasons, by its assurance of the presence of the Eternal in time, by breaking through the endless cycles and seasons of life and history leading to some natural end and lifting us out of a hopeless endurance.

Be at work in us, our Father, that new life may follow seasons of cold, that hope may drive out the dark of despair. Through Christ our Lord. Amen.

WEEK 41

I will be with you.—Isa. 43:2

God's Not Killed

Week 41——Day 1   **Read Acts 27:13-26**

To someone caught in a frightful tempest, not of wind and wave, but of fear or temptation, this passage brings sustaining reminder. Paul's words come to us across the years, "Take heart. . . . Do not be afraid." Just as God cared about what happened to Paul on that voyage to Rome, "you must stand before Caesar," so God cares about what happens to each of us in the storms in which we are now caught. No one can say how it will come out, but God is in it with us as he was with Paul, needing and wanting our safety.

In one of the underground caves in the beseiged city of Vicksburg in 1863 a child was crying. Her mother said, "Don't cry, my darling. God will protect us." The child sobbed,

"Mama, I'm so 'fraid God's killed, too." God was not killed then—nor now.

Our Father, grant us courage, wisdom, hope, and trust, in all the storms that put us in peril. In the Spirit of Christ. Amen.

Week 41——Day 2   Read Isa. 43:1-7

Joseph Fort Newton tells of being in a London theater during the war when a British Tommy asked him, "What is the grace of God?" Before he could answer, a New Zealander broke in with this: "The grace of God is like the ever-present healing power of healing in nature. When we are pinked [slang for wounded] all the forces of health in the body are rushed to that spot to repair the damage. In the spiritual world a power of healing is always at work, if we let it have its way and work with it."

One could scarcely put it better than that. Will we let the healing, recuperative powers of God work with us this day?

Come, Holy Spirit, to heal the wounds of life that are beyond our help and to bind up into wholeness what we cannot mend. For Christ's sake. Amen.

Week 41——Day 3   Read Ezek. 1:1-3

This day will find untold numbers of people far from home or preparing for some journey to a distant place. Ezekiel's experience offers both instruction and encouragement. He was in a far country, away from easy familiarity with custom and demand, lonely and homesick. There in the distant exile he saw a vision of God. God is present at every river Chebar where some traveler from home awaits him with faith this day. As it was to Ezekiel, so may it be to us on all our life's journeys: "By the river Chebar . . . I saw visions of God."

Thanks be to thee, God, that to every place we journey thou wilt come thyself. Through Christ our Lord. Amen.

Week 41——Day 4   Read Deut. 26:16-19

Wonderful words for meditation come from Alistair MacLean's *High Country:* "A multitude of things there are we cannot do. The past is folded in the book of God. The future is fast hidden in the heart of God. But today is ours, and Truth and Love and Goodness and Fellowship and Freedom. Surely the gift of today is sufficient to take the sting from yesterday and fear from tomorrow." True—on one condition! That we face today in the power of God's promise that we are a people holy to him.

Praise be to thee, O Lord, for this day. Let us not spoil it either by remorse for yesterday or anxiety for tomorrow, for thou art with us today. In Jesus' name. Amen.

Week 41——Day 5   Read Gen. 28:10-15

With this story in mind William Hazlitt made the prophecy, "There can never be another Jacob's dream. Since that time, the heavens have gone farther off, and grown astronomical." The obvious truth of these words is disturbing at first. Astronomy has put an end to such dreams. But while the heavens may have gone farther off, God has not moved away. If God is truly the Lord of heaven and earth, ever abounding in steadfast love, does it matter the "size" of creation? Jacob dreamed

187

of a God who said, "I am with you." Astronomy does not change that.

Thou art high and lifted up, O Lord, but thou dwellest also in the humble and contrite heart. Through Jesus Christ our Lord. Amen.

Week 41——Day 6   Read Ps. 139:1-6

In James Barrie's *A Window in Thrums* the young man, Joey, about to become a minister, is suddenly killed in a traffic accident. His first sermon was to have been on the text, "Thou, God, seest me" (Gen. 16:13 K.J.V.). Twenty years later his mother tells of it, "Ay, but that day he was coffined, for all the minister prayed, I found it hard to say, 'Thou, God, seest me.' It's the text I like best noo . . . I turn't up often in the Bible . . . for aince a body's sure o' that, they're sure o' all."

Help us, our Father, to be sure that thou art acquainted with all our ways, yet lovest us still. In Jesus' name. Amen.

Week 41——Day 7   Read Isa. 41:10

"Fear not, for I am with you." Twenty-one times in the Bible this exact promise is made—and how many times more is it given in parallel words! We pass through no deep waters unaccompanied nor any fire unprotected.

This assurance is great comfort in times of trouble and need. There is no darkness where God cannot and will not find us. This promise is substantial support in times when our strength is insufficient. To endeavors beyond all human powers we can ask God to lend his aid. This pledge is wonderful incentive to reach for the highest, to try for the best, and to spurn unholy contentments.

Sometimes our lives are not worthy for thee to know, O God. But abide with us, even so, and make us true and strong, clean and unafraid. For Jesus' sake. Amen.

WEEK 42

The life was the light of men.—John 1:4

Fearless, Happy, and in Constant Trouble

Week 42——Day 1   **Read Luke 6:20-31**

There is much in these verses to provoke a kind of *holy fear;* suffice it to consider verses 24 to 26. William Barclay put the inescapable question thus: "Will you be happy in the world's way, or in Christ's way?" F. R. Maltby said, "Jesus promised his disciples three things—that they would be completely fearless, absurdly happy and in constant trouble." Woe to me if I should ever be full with the world's rewards of goods, honors, and praise. Then I would neither desire nor seek what Christ offers—trouble, tears, and above all, God.

Woe is me if this day seems complete without thee, O God. Save me from any comfort or satisfaction that kills. In Jesus' name. Amen.

From the top of East Rock above New Haven, Connecticut, one can trace the route of the Connecticut Turnpike by its blue-white lights. A spectacular string of shining lights marks the way of the turnpike across the city in the night, through deep blackness, through the glitter and glare of other lights. Always the way of the turnpike is clear. So Jesus marks his way across all the world and down the darkness of history, through the gaudy glare of the lights that we make. He is bright illumination through the darkest nights of earth and unmistakable path across the glare of our world.

O Light of the world, shine for us with a radiance no darkness can put out. In thy name. Amen.

Frederick II, medieval emperor, once made this confession: "I have followed Aristotle only when his opinions have been confirmed by my own observations." It could scarcely matter less whether Frederick went along with Aristotle. Nothing could hardly matter more than that we go along with Christ and what God has revealed in him. Yet our attitude is commonly the same; we follow only what has been confirmed to our own observation. But does our observation see far enough? To test all truth in experience is good, but to say that God cannot lead us, "the blind," in a path we know not, by ways yet untrod, may be to miss his way altogether.

By faith, O Christ, we make thy love the test of every way and thy life the test of every truth. In thy name. Amen.

Scientists have discovered a "new kind of light" called "laser." One of its incredible properties is to travel infinitely without "spreading," as ordinary light does. By means of this light communications can be sent throughout the universe when men journey out beyond earth. The other amazing property of laser is that it is able to carry all the messages being sent anywhere in the world simultaneously. Is there not parallel truth here to the image, Christ, the Light of the world? Faith proclaims that God's truth as we see it in Jesus Christ will carry to the uttermost reaches of space, and Christ can carry the burden of all the world's hopes and fears.

We thank thee, God, for thy light shining in Christ to support all mystery and to journey with us through all space and time. In his name. Amen.

Jesus came as the light of the world. Those who call themselves his disciples ought to reflect his light for others to see in the dark places of the world. A Christian can be committed to no higher purpose than to letting the light shine through him and from him. Sassoon put this purpose with beauty in one of his poems: "You that keep in a land asleep, one light burning till break of day." In a land where people sleep, indifferent to human need, the follower of Jesus will keep the light of Christlike concern burning. In a community or family where fear hovers like a heavy cloud the person of faith will keep the light of faith shining.

Goodspeed translated Phil. 2:15: Christians should "appear like stars in a dark world." People need light to find their way in the darkness of each day. What light of hope, judgment, encouragement, or faith shines in, through, and from us?

Let thy light shine through us that none within our sight may be lost. For Jesus' sake. Amen.

Week 42——Day 6   Read Acts 17:11

In 1931 editor Lincoln Steffens told how he had decided to read the New Testament to see what good churchgoing Christians believed.

The experience was an adventure so startling that I wanted everybody else to have it; I still recommend people to read the New Testament as I read it, without reverence, with feet up on a desk and a pipe in the mouth, as news. It is news. It made the stuff I was writing in the magazine old stuff. All my stories of all the cities and states were one story . . . and these were all in that old story of Christ.

Whether one reads it with or without reverence the Bible is more timely news than the front page of tomorrow's paper. The truth of all that is in the paper is written in the Book.

Let the scripture speak to us as news, O God, news of thy purpose and thy mighty acts telling us truth about ourselves. In Jesus' name. Amen.

Week 42——Day 7   Read Acts 3:1-10

A traveler to any part of the Middle East hears one word more than all others—*baksheesh*. It is the cry of the beggar. So might the beggar in this chapter have cried to Peter and John. "He fixed his attention upon them—*baksheesh*—expecting to receive something from them." Are we not most of us like that beggar, crying *baksheesh* to Christ, to his disciples, or to the church? What do we expect—some kind of blessing or favor or security? The gift Christ offers is so much more. He gives us the capacity to arise and walk from the paralysis of prejudice, greed, and fear into new life.

O God, at thy touch let our baksheesh *turn to praise. In Christ's name. Amen.*

WEEK 43

I will remember their sin no more.—Jer. 31:34

Forget It!

Week 43——Day 1   Read Isa. 43:25

To Isaiah came the word of God, "I will not remember your sins." If God is willing to forget my sins I ought to forget them too. Once a person has repented of his evil he should be done with it, put it behind him, and call it to remembrance no more. What a denial of faith to declare our trust in a God who forgives and forgets, yet to carry on with us through life a vast burden of unforgiven sin! "Forget it!" is faithful advice. Forget it, not in casual disregard, but in penitent turning from past sin to present hope in the Savior's love.

Help us this day to remember thy promise of forgiveness and be released from our sinful past. For Jesus' sake. Amen.

Week 43——Day 2   Read Luke 23:39-43

Somehow the penitent thief felt the authority and power of Jesus and saw in him a hope that reached clear down to the bottom of his despair. "Jesus, remember me." Jesus answered in words whose echo has never died, "Today you will be with me in Paradise." It means more than any of us can ever figure that this criminal was in the crucifixion. We all walk the way he went, bearing with us the weight of wrong and sin. Only a God who can come across the darkness to us on our side can take it away. On Calvary's summit Christ demonstrated that God does that.

Jesus, in thy kingly power, remember us in our needs. For thy mercy's sake. Amen.

Week 43——Day 3   Read Rom. 8:31-32

With a slab taken from the old Coventry Cathedral, destroyed by German bombs in the war, an altar has been built in the open ruins. Above this altar is a dramatic cross made from charred beams lashed together the morning after the air raids. Behind the cross two words have been engraved on the wall, "Father, forgive."

He did not spare his own Son but gave him up for us all." As disciples of the Christ we must forgive each other, using even the broken things of life to show our forgiveness.

Toward any who have hurt us, O God, may we this day offer

*the forgiveness of Christ in the spirit of the cross. For his sake.
Amen.*

Week 43——Day 4   Read Hos. 7:1-2; 8:7

Archbishop William Temple once observed: "The world is
always asking the Church to tell it how it can escape the consequences of its sin. . . . But the Church ought to have no
interest in doing this. Its concern is to tell men how to escape
from sin itself." Hosea understood long ago that the consequences of sin cannot be escaped. A price is always paid
by someone. "Sow the wind . . . reap the whirlwind." He is
a foolish man who sows his wild oats and prays for a crop failure.

Remembering Hosea's words we ask with Paul, "Who shall
deliver us from this death in our sins?"

*Thanks be to thee, O God. Through our Lord Jesus Christ.
Amen.*

Week 43——Day 5   Read Rom. 7:21-25

The famous *Twelve Steps to Recovery* of Alcoholics Anonymous offer guidance to any person fighting a battle with spiritual evil of whatever kind:

1. We admitted we were powerless over (alcohol)—that our
lives had become unmanageable.
2. We came to believe that a Power greater than ourselves could
restore us to sanity.

3. We made a decision to turn our will and our lives over to the care of God *as we understood Him.*

4. We made a searching and fearless moral inventory of ourselves.

5. We admitted to God, to ourselves, and to another human being the exact nature of our wrongs.

6. We were entirely ready to have God remove all these defects of character.

Whether our evil be alcohol or anger, lust or lethargy, idolatry or indifference, we cannot win the battle alone. We need God, and we need at least one other human helper.

Let no fear keep us from confession, our Father, for a contrite heart thou wilt not despise, but help. In Jesus' name. Amen.

Week 43——Day 6   Read Ps. 107:1-22

The remaining steps in the A.A. program are these:

7. We humbly asked God to remove our shortcomings.

8. We became willing to make amends to all the persons we had harmed.

9. We made direct amends to such people whenever possible, except when to do so would injure them or others.

10. We continued to take personal inventory and when we were wrong we promptly admitted it.

11. We sought through prayer and meditation to improve our conscious contact with God, praying only for knowledge of his will for us and power to carry that out.

12. Having had a spiritual awakening as a result of these steps, we tried to carry this message to (alcoholics) and to practice these principles in our lives.

Notice the recurring refrain in Ps. 107:

> Then they cried to the Lord in their trouble,
> and he delivered them from their distress.

This is the secret of victory over sin—receiving the steadfast love which God offers.

Let thy renewing word heal us and deliver us, O God of redeeming love. Through Christ. Amen.

Week 43——Day 7   Read Ps. 130

Martin Luther called this one of the four greatest psalms in the Psalter. Anyone who has ever been through the pangs of remorse, the anguish of begging forgiveness of God, or of another person, would never dispute Luther's judgment. From the deepest depths into which it is possible to fall—not being right with God—we cry for help. Our separation from God cannot be covered, any more than the Grand Canyon can be covered. The more we love him the more we know how far we have fallen. It is as though we lay with a broken leg at the bottom of some Grand Canyon of evil and cried to the rim for help. Someone must come for us! This psalmist knows the God whose plenitude of mercy will lift him up restored to the joy of his presence.

Our hope is not in ourselves, O God, but in thee, to lift us out of the deep places into which our own destructive hearts have cast us. Through Christ our Lord. Amen.

WEEK 44

Thanks be to God.—I Cor. 15:57

Whose Love Is the Story of My Life

Week 44——Day 1   **Read Gal. 2:20**

Helen Keller dedicated one of her books: "To Anne Sullivan, whose love is the story of my life." How many of us would say that of someone who made the great difference in life for us? Someone's love is the story of every life that finds itself in the way God intended that it should. How many might say the same of Jesus Christ! His love is *the* story of their lives. No day passes that they do not give thanks for him who loved them and gave himself for them. Christ's love is the story of the best we have ever been or done.

Thanks be to thee, O God, for thine inestimable love declared unto us. Through Jesus Christ our Lord. Amen.

Week 44——Day 2   **Read Acts 26:19-23; 28:30-31**

Of Thomas Hart Benton, distinguished senator from Missouri in the mid-nineteenth century, his biographer, Theodore Roosevelt, said: "He is one of the very few men in our history who have passed out of mortal view still rising." What a wonderful tribute to be paid to anyone, that to the very end he could be "rising"—doing his noblest work, speaking his finest words. Paul qualified for such praise. The scriptures we read in the book of Acts leave us no doubt of that.

How much do you owe of life and faith and joy to someone

perhaps unknown by the world but greatly loved by you who when he passed from mortal view was still rising?

I thank thee, God, for one who was true to the very best, to the very last, and now dwells in thee. In Jesus' name. Amen.

Week 44——Day 3   Read John 4:38; I Cor. 7:23

We are remiss in handling sacred trust if we do not find a quiet period in each day, however brief it must be, to reflect upon these two verses reminding us of the debts we owe. How many others have labored in our behalf that we could come to this hour –parents, friends, colleagues, children, partners, teachers, martyrs, and heroes of the race! Think of them now, one by one. All that we have, all that we are, has been bought with enormous price. We are not our own. We were bought with a price none may repay. Let us be grateful.

We thank thee, God, for the life laid down, the preference given up, the love poured out for us. In Jesus' name. Amen.

Week 44——Day 4   Read Acts 3:24-26

André Malraux once wrote, "A heritage is not transmitted: it must be conquered." So—the faith of our fathers is not ours by inheritance; it is ours only by our own faith. We must win through doubt and temptation, even as did the great ones who broke the way for us. They have made it easier because they have gone on ahead—Moses, Elijah, Jeremiah, Jesus, Paul, and all the saints and prophets who preceded us. We are in the great succession, thank God! But as Jean Jaures admonished, "We must take from the past its fires, not its ashes."

Let the flame of thy Spirit touch our souls till we win the inheritance of our fathers' faith, O Lord. In Christ's name. Amen.

Week 44——Day 5   Read Col. 1:11-14

Bernard DeVoto believes that the greatest contribution of the Lewis and Clark expedition was that it gave the entire West to the American people as "something the mind could deal with." Hitherto this void had been a region of rumor, guess, and fantasy. After Lewis and Clark, however, "the mind could focus on reality." Christians say the same of their saints, renowned and obscure, who explored all the lands of human fear and Christian trust. Because the saints have gone before us we are delivered from the dominion of darkness.

Thanks be to thee, O God, for the witness of faithful souls in whose light we see light and by whose examples we are enabled to walk in paths of righteousness. For Christ's sake. Amen.

Week 44——Day 6   Read John 16:4

In *Sometime Never* Clare Leighton paid tribute to her memories for their beneficent power of healing, for serving as "an unassailable defense when the hysteria of heightened emotion explodes within us the tension that binds this storm-threatened world." She finds them balm, too, for "the trivial fret of life."

God has been gracious to us in times gone by. Has he not given healing for hurt, forgiveness for failure, hope for discouragement? Love, joy, and peace have crowned many of our days. There should be balm in the remembrance of these mercies, and in the thought that the God who so blessed the past is with us still, and will be with us in the hard days to come.

Thanks be to thee, O God, for all gracious, healing memories. In Jesus' name. Amen.

Week 44——Day 7 Read Lam. 3:22-23

What strange words to find in a book of lamentations. We would lament if they were not true. They are true, however, and their truth alters the whole face of life. No matter what the day before has brought, with each new day comes a new store of God's lovingkindness. True, each day must be the product of the days preceding it. No less true, each day is truly a *new* day. If today were just the deposit of all our yesterdays— how ghastly the prospect! But in each new day is the recurring constant of God's steadfast love. He can make something new of old patterns. We can make a fresh start in this day, and again tomorrow, and on all our tomorrows, knowing that God's mercy is never exhausted.

Thy love rises for us, O God, with the sun, new every morning. In Jesus' name. Amen.

WEEK 45

Mary, the Mother of Jesus

Week 45——Day 1   **Read Luke 2:41-51**

This is the first of seven pictures through which we shall look at Mary, the mother of Jesus hoping to find in her life a helpful testament of faith. Mary is naturally baffled by Jesus' unexpected behavior: "Why have you treated us so?" A strange spirit seems already to possess her Son: "I must be in my Father's house." Yet Mary is open to the truth whatever the truth may be. She kept all these things in her heart. She must have sensed that in some way God was calling her Son to a divine purpose. She kept that thought nearest her heart and let it be the guide for her life.

We would keep in our hearts every intimation of thy purpose for us and those we love. For Jesus' sake. Amen.

Week 45——Day 2   **Read John 2:1-12**

"Woman, what have you to do with me?" It sounds abrupt, even discourteous. This is only because we have no English word to render the meaning of honor and love which the Greek word carries. May we not hear this as Jesus telling his mother that she does not understand either the new wine which will be in the stone jars or the new wine of his mission and message? But when "his time comes" all will be revealed.

In the meantime Mary must trust him in the use of God's power.

O Christ, neither thy way with God's power nor thy purposes with us are always clear. Yet we would trust the integrity of thy love. Amen.

Week 45——Day 3   Read Mark 3:20-35

When Jesus' family came to get hold of him did Mary, too, doubt his sanity? Or did she come to temper the unpleasant purpose and encounter with compassion? We do not know. But Jesus was pointing here to a new concept of family. Mary must share the relationship of mother with all others who loved God. Such stretching of family ties must have disturbed her, as it does us, but she allowed God's love to win over any limits that anyone would have put upon it.

Let us thus behave this day, our Father, as devoted members of Christ's family. For his sake. Amen.

Week 45——Day 4   Read John 19:25-27

Elizabeth Peabody was once asked how she happened to run into a tree on the Boston Common. She replied, "I saw it but I did not realize it." A world of difference sometimes lies between seeing and realizing. Mary may have seen long since what awaited her Son. Here on Calvary she realized it. Now anguish and death were altogether real. In such a moment Mary found a divine love that could see her life through. In such moments, when our love is crucified, then we find God's love in fullest measure.

Help us, our Father, to realize thy love that never lets us go; so may our love never fail anyone whom thou hast given to us. For Christ's sake. Amen.

Week 45——Day 5   Read Acts 1:12-14

We have no record in the New Testament that Jesus "appeared" to his mother in the way of his appearances to his disciples and others. It may be that she was one of the blessed of whom Jesus spoke to Thomas—"who have not seen and yet believe." At any rate here is Mary and Jesus' brothers in the Apostolic company full of faith in the resurrection, devoted to prayer, taking up the task of being witnesses for Jesus in the world. Mary's testament is that God offers a love able to see us through the very worst and then confirm us in the holy tasks of doing his will.

Come what may, we would trust thee, O God; set us now to thy holy purposes. In Jesus' name. Amen.

Week 45——Day 6   Read Matt. 1:18-21

"You shall call his name Jesus, for he will save his people from their sins." Matthew wrote this account of the annunciation many years after the resurrection when the entire good news was known. It had by then become clear what God was doing in this affair—saving his people from their sin. Whether this was fully known by Mary before or during Jesus' life is not important. What is important is that Mary allowed herself to be used by God for his greatest purposes of love.

Let us also be instruments for thy saving love, undiscour-

ageable in the love which goes beyond sin. For Christ's sake. Amen.

> He who is mighty has done great things for me,
> and holy is his name.

In the light of all that Luke knew when he wrote his Gospel these words are even more true than Mary could possibly have known at any time before the resurrection. They are great words to ponder—that he who is Lord of creation does great things for one whose humility will allow it. God does regard each one of his children, however low may be his estate. His mercy is on us all. For this great truth, which was revealed here to Mary in a new way, we thank God, and follow her in our devotion.

My soul magnifies the Lord, and my spirit rejoices in thee, my Savior. Through Jesus Christ. Amen.

What does the Lord require?
You shall be my witnesses.—Acts 1:8

Your Religion Is Showing

Week 46——Day 1   Read Matt. 5-16

George H. Tolley told of the Girl Scout leader who was pulled up sharply by the remark of one of her smallest scouts. They had completed a strenuous hike and were resting when the child noticed that the leader's religious medal which she, as a good Roman Catholic, always wore was hanging outside her uniform. Said the little girl, "Your religion is showing."

Our faith ought to show, even more in the example of living than in visible insignia. What do we do in our daily affairs that would cause anyone to think or say, "Your religion is showing"?

May our light, which has its source in thee, O God, shine brightly and so encourage others to give thee glory. In Christ's name. Amen.

Week 46——Day 2   Read Zech. 8:20-23

Has anyone ever seized your coat saying, "Let us go with you, for we have heard that God is with you"? What would make another person believe God was with you? Joy that does not flinch at sorrow because it knows that God can redeem all sorrow? Pity that knows no bounds to its reach? Forgiveness that nurses no resentments? Inner peace for the facing of this hour and the living of these days that only God could give? Courage to stand for goodness in the evil day?

Lord, let me so bear myself this day that others will see and wish to join me in faith. In Jesus' name. Amen.

Week 46——Day 3   Read Acts 23:1-10

Paul said, "I did not know . . . he was the high priest." Did he not see him? Perhaps he was not presiding, but there only as a spectator. The words have a disturbing irony in them which Paul himself may have intended. How would anyone possibly know that this man was the high priest? He sat in judgment according to the law; yet he broke the law. In other words, he gave an unrecognizable witness to that of which he was high priest.

Will any have occasion to say of us this day, "I did not know he was a Christian"? As someone recently remarked of a man's failure with a moral issue, "The only statements that counted were those that were made loud and clear before the whole world."

Let our faith be clearly seen, O God, and our commitment unmistakably recognized in the way we conduct the affairs of this day. In Jesus' name. Amen.

Week 46——Day 4   Read Acts 26:19-32

"Not done in a corner." I should say not! Can you even imagine Paul hiding his faith in a corner? That's the trouble with a good deal of Christianity; we practice it in a corner, keeping it hushed up so as not to attract attention. But what good is a *witness* if people don't see it? Charles Peguy said: "He who does not bellow the truth when he knows the truth makes himself the accomplice of liars and forgers." We can be sure that some will think we are crazy. We can be sure that sometimes we will be wrong. None will doubt, however, that we are obedient to a vision larger and better than ourselves.

Forbid, O God of truth, that our faith in thee should ever escape notice by those who know us. In Jesus' name. Amen.

Week 46——Day 5   Read Matt. 5:16

Some years ago a remarkable picture appeared in a popular magazine showing a whole neighborhood lighted by flashbulbs successively discharged in front of each house. The city is a blaze of glory, but each home is lighted by a single flash. One thinks back to those earliest days of the lighting of London when every evening the lamplighter knocked on each door with the command, "Hang out your light!" There are dark streets and dark corners where we live that only our light of faith will illumine.

O God, let our lights so shine that none will stumble in darkness where we are. Through Jesus Christ. Amen.

Week 46——Day 6   Read Acts 19:11-20

I thank God today for an evil spirit! That is not blasphemy; I refer to the evil spirit in the man who leaped on the sons of Sceva crying, "Jesus I know, and Paul I know; but who are you?" I am grateful to this demon for asking the question I dare not forget, "Who are you?" It is never enough for me to be a Christian by the name of Jesus whom Paul preaches, or anyone else. I must witness by the power of the Jesus who has changed *my* life. Evil has scant fear of hearsay—only first-hand encounter with Christ threatens the power of evil.

Break through my words to appear also in my life, O Spirit of the risen Christ. In his name. Amen.

Week 46——Day 7   **Read I Tim. 4:11-16**

Around the time of the Civil War rustic audiences arriving at Salt Lake City marveled at the material advances and culture which they found in the Mormon capital. They did not know what to make of Dumas' tragedy *Camille* when it was presented in the theater. In the final act, when the dying Camille is convulsed by coughing, a sympathetic elderly lady walked to the stage with a glass of water. That is what one might call audience response. Would that our Christian witness were as convincing, that people would respond as much to the life which we gave to the faith as those audiences responded to the acting of tragedy upon a stage.

May we so devote ourselves to Christian practice that others will believe we mean it. For Christ's sake. Amen.

What does the Lord require?
Whoever does the will of God.—Mark 3:35

I Will Not Be My Own Follower

Week 47——Day 1   **Read Luke 19:1-10**

The story of Zacchaeus is the story of a man who got out of a revolving door and set out on a great journey. When Jesus came to his house he woke up to what he had done, and even more important, what he had missed. He became a new man, no longer pledged to himself but sworn to a greater allegiance.

Many people are like nothing so much as foolish dogs chasing their own tails. Round and round they go in pursuit of themselves, never moving off to seek great purposes and unselfish ambitions. Karl Barth, commenting on his "disciples," once remarked half humorously that he refused to become his own follower. It is a good resolution for any person to make. Don't become your own follower. Let God set you free from the revolving door of preconceived ideas and the spinning circle of narrow loyalties.

Shake us loose from the confining restriction of our own ideas, our Father, and call us to venture forth in the lively and saving ways of Jesus. For his sake. Amen.

Week 47——Day 2   **Read Matt. 26:42**

"Thy will be done"—these are great words of acceptance. Far too often we reserve them for moments when all choice has been taken from us. When there's nothing more we can do we resign ourselves to the will of God, sometimes dishonestly, for if there were anything else we could do we would do it. It is as though we say to God: "You have me where I can't escape. It's your will, no matter what, so let it be done." Jesus did not wait until he was on the cross to say "Thy will be done." He said it in Gethsemane—in the garden of decision.

May our resignation to thy will, our Father, be not forced but ours by deliberate choice. For Christ's sake. Amen.

Week 47——Day 3   Read Matt. 6:10

Auto accidents, death from agonizing disease, and all devastating calamities are *not* God's will—at least not his intentional will, although they happen by his permission. That we must make moral choices of goodness instead of evil God does intend. In moments when we still possess some choice and freedom of action, to say, "Thy righteous will be done," is a mark of spiritual power. Thy will be done in race relations— let me do the right thing, painful though it be. Thy will be done in forgiveness—let me humble myself though it hurts. Thy will be done in commitment of life—whatever I must deny myself.

Today, my Father, let me do thy will in all things to which I commit myself. In Jesus' name. Amen.

Week 47——Day 4   Read Job 42:5

Someone has said that if in the next world we should come to a fork in the road with a sign pointing one way: *To Heaven,*

211

and another the opposite way: *To Lectures About Heaven,* most Americans would choose the latter road. We love to know all about things, especially things religious. We are less enthusiastic about actually becoming involved in these things. How much time have we spent this week talking, hearing, reading *about* the faith? And how much time personally involved with *doing the will of God?*

O Lord, hearing of thee by our ears, having ideas about thee with our minds will not do. Move us to love thee this day by some commitment to thy will. For Christ's sake. Amen.

Week 47——Day 5   Read John 6:35

A visitor from Asia remarked on the white bread Americans eat, that so many of the nutrients are removed from the flour. "Yes," said his host, "but we like the taste so much better than whole wheat." Fortunately the white bread is now synthetically enriched so these values are restored, but there is a parable here for our understanding. We also like to bleach out so many of the nutrients of Christ, the bread of life. He "tastes" better if his harder sayings about judgment and discipline are bleached out. There is no way to eat the true bread of life except we eat it whole.

O God, restrain us from bleaching out the gospel to suit our personal taste. Make plain that we cannot half do thy will. Feed us with the whole Christ that we may be strong to do thy will. For Jesus' sake. Amen.

Life should be shaken when we pray. One real test as to whether prayer has reached its mark and gained a response from God is whether life is in any way shaken up to become different in consequence. John Hunt, the missionary to the Fiji Islands, told about once when the steam was up in the launch ready for the day's journey and he called on a local preacher to lead in prayer. The man prayed earnestly for twenty minutes. When he had risen from his knees the native engineer looked at the steam gauge and said quietly, "That brother has prayed forty pounds of pressure off the boiler. We shall have to make it up again before we start."

Prayer ought to relieve some pressures. Others it must generate until we are shaken loose from our moorings to get on with God's work.

Let our prayers be not merely blowing off of steam but the generation of power and purpose to do thy will. For Jesus' sake. Amen.

Henri Amiel, Swiss poet and philosopher, among the last entries in his famous *Journal*, wrote words of perception whose truth none can afford to miss: "What dupes we are of our own desires! . . . Destiny has two ways of crushing us—by refusing our wishes and by fulfilling them. But he who only wills what God wills escapes both catastrophes. All things work together for his good." Let us beware lest we have our reward by desiring the wrong thing—and having the desire fulfilled.

Let thy will be done in all things, O God, that we be not crushed but fulfilled through thy holy purpose. For Christ's sake. Amen.

WEEK 48

Here I am! Send me.—Isa. 6:8

Lift Anchor and Sail

Week 48——Day 1   **Read Matt. 7:21**

A wise man once made the observation, "If a ship is going to ride at anchor till she rots, it doesn't make a straw's difference whether her chart and compass are false or true." This truth is so obvious as to be often overlooked. The parallel is no less obvious and as frequently missed. If a life never cuts its anchor and sets out into the great waters of Christian discipleship, it makes not a straw's difference if it be filled with piety and sound doctrine. The great thing is to *do* God's will. By what lines are we held to the anchor? By what Spirit will we have grace to lift the anchor and sail?

May I this day lift anchor and set sail on some great business of thy kingdom, O God. For Jesus' sake. Amen.

We sometimes see the deepest meaning of scripture if we try to imagine how an event *might* have happened if the people concerned had acted differently. Suppose, for example, this is the way things had gone: "And the jailer said, 'Splendid! I'll be baptized some time later, as soon as these troubles are over.' After Paul had been publicly released by the magistrate and had departed, the jailer was glad to return to his former life. He saw no need then to be baptized." That is how we might have done it, thinking it best to wait until things had quieted down and we had seen what all the effect would be. Thank God the jailer acted immediately in response to God's goodness, for we have his witness to remind us that the time to answer God's appeal is in the moment when it comes.

So be it even for us, O God. In the Spirit of Christ. Amen.

When Michael Faraday was a boy he sold newspapers to earn his living. One day while waiting outside the office of an Edinburgh paper for the morning issue he thrust his head and arms through the railings of the iron gate. "Now my head and hands are on one side, my heart and body on the other," he said to himself. "Which side of the gate am I on?" The gate was suddenly opened; the wrench he received taught him a lesson. The head, hands, heart, and body must all be on one side. It is no good to praise God with the lips if we do not serve him with heart and body.

Father, may we always stand altogether on thy side of every fence or choice. In Jesus' name. Amen.

"At ease in Zion"—this is a danger sign, said Amos. If I am altogether comfortable in my faith I had better watch out! In his caution against casual Christianity J. A. Davidson of England refers to the cartoon in *The New Yorker* showing a couple obviously "enjoying" a religious service on TV while they lounge in the living room. The door bell rings and upon opening the front door the man sees an usher from the church holding out a collection plate. At a deeper level of seriousness, beneath the humor of the man's consternation, this drives home the point that God tries to disturb the casual ease of our faith—not just with the "nuisance" of a collection, but with the unrelenting demand for a life. "Behold I stand at the door [of your ease] and knock," said the Lord.

Disturb our ease in thee, O God. Let us find no enjoyment in faith until we know the joy of response to thy will. In Jesus Christ our Lord. Amen.

When the Viennese pianist Paul Wittgenstein lost his right arm during World War I he refused to abandon his ambition to be a concert artist. He built up a special repertory around his handicap—works written especially for him by such composers as Richard Strauss, Paul Hindemith, Benjamin Britten, and Maurice Ravel. He strengthened what remained, found resources of inspiration in what would have been improperly called his handicap. By consecrating his weakness to the best for which it could be used he did wonderful things for music. His example is strong reminder that God's power is made perfect in our weakness.

Praise be to thee, O God, that thou canst use even the weakness which we consecrate to thee for glorious purpose. Through Jesus Christ. Amen.

Week 48——Day 6   Read Matt. 10:38-39

Rudyard Kipling once wrote about the years he lived in Brattleboro, Vermont: "And so four years passed and a good deal of verse and prose saw the light. Better than all, I had known a corner of the United States as a householder, which is the only way of getting at a country. Tourists may carry away impressions, but it is the seasonal detail of small things."

Has he not observed what is also true of Christian understanding? How can one ever know what it means to love God and to serve the cause of Christ except as a householder—except as one who lives within the faith and discipline of Christian life? "Religious tourists" can have only impressions, and these are seasonal details. We must *move in* and *take up residence.*

Help us, O God, to make our true dwelling within the demands and promises of Christ. In his Spirit. Amen.

Week 48——Day 7   Read Ps. 127:1; John 3:3

Life is altogether conditional. All things demand their price. The word "unless" attaches to every promise, qualifies every great hope. One of the first demands every new experience makes on a person is that he read on through the "small print."

"Unless the Lord build the house. . . ." No one builds a house where love endures who does not build it on the love of God, on the faith that all personality is sacred because God loves it.

"Unless one is born anew. . . ." Unless I reorient my whole life so that it is held in moral orbit by the pull of God's righteousness I will not see his Kingdom.

O God, make me to consider all thy promises and to know the conditions of all thy blessings. In Jesus' name. Amen.

WEEK 49

I was not disobedient to the heavenly vision.—Acts 26:19

The Saving Word Is "Yes"

Week 49——Day 1   **Read Matt. 4:18-22**

Bennet Cerf recounted the story of the young banker who picked up the telephone in his office. His end of the conversation went as follows: "No . . . NO . . . no . . . no . . . no . . . YES . . . no . . . NO!" With a final explosive no he hung up.

The head of the firm overheard him and chided, "What was the idea of saying 'Yes' to that fellow?"

"I had to," answered his junior morosely. "He asked me if I could hear him.'

God was not on the other end of that phone. But the story suggests a truth. When God asks, the saving word is "Yes."

Lord, help me to speak it today. For Jesus' sake. Amen.

In a paper saved from World War II I find this headline, *The Greeks in the Blackout*. It referred to a discussion in Britain as to what one should read during the blackouts. The opinion was that what is required is the lucid and the resolved. "One needs a detachment that at the same time is not an evasion." Living in our world with its massive threats, we still feel this need. We need to spend some moments of each day detached from the chaos of existence, in prayer, reading, hearing great music. This is not an evasion, but makes it possible for us to come back in strength from the "heavenly vision" resolved to be responsible. Jesus came down from the hills and stood level with a great crowd.

Draw us to thyself, O God, that we may stand again in thy purpose level with the world. For Christ's sake. Amen.

Pass at Your Own Risk. This familiar sign warns us in places of possible peril. Beyond this limit is danger! God has marked the moral highway of our going with such signs. "You shall not eat of the tree of the knowledge of good and evil." Pass at your own risk. You will try to make yourself God rather than creature at your own moral peril. As we have discovered! "You shall not covet." Pass at your own risk. See what covetousness has done to us! Usually we are not stopped by road blocks on the way to self-destruction. Because we are morally free God can only warn us.

We would dwell in thought this day on thy warning words,

O God, to be sure that we cannot pass the allowance of thy love without danger. In Jesus' name. Amen.

Week 49——Day 4   Read II Cor. 3:4-6

"Fidelity is to the spirit, not to the letter; though *you cannot kill the letter and keep the spirit.*" This observation by a scholar on the perils of translating the scriptures applies with force to our moral and spiritual life as well. Paul was right; in matters of faith and obedience "the written code kills, but the Spirit gives life." The peril for us, however, is more likely to be that we will play fast and loose with rules and promises, saying, "We're acting in the *spirit* of the thing"—only to discover that by ignoring the letter we have killed the spirit.

Save us from disregard of law, rule, and discipline, our Father, but let the spirit of our obedience give life to the letter. In Jesus' name. Amen.

Week 49——Day 5   Read Matt. 6:34

The great William Osler, medical pioneer, attributed his success to following out a sentence of Thomas Carlyle which he read as a young medical student. "Our main business is not to see what lies dimly at a distance, but to do what lies clearly at hand." Osler used to advise his students to live in "day-tight compartments."

It is a good rule to follow. Plan and provide what you may or must for the dim future in the light of the heavenly vision as you have seen it, but seek God's daily help to do what each day requires.

Grant us thy grace, our Father, to discharge with honor the duties of this day, confident that both yesterday and tomorrow are secure in thy keeping. In Jesus' name. Amen.

Week 49——Day 6   **Read Eph. 4:25-27**

"A world filled with trapdoors into chaos" was the headline describing the subject of a recent book. Can you think of a more accurate description of the world we live in? Consider some of the trapdoors into chaos: Trying to maintain a way of life where some are deprived of rights because of nationality, religion, political conviction, or color of skin; imagining that we can violate the moral sanctities and not hurt someone; thinking we can neglect prayer and the spiritual life and yet have resources against the days of adversity; practicing small infidelities and fraud and expecting no later consequences. What opportunities we are giving to the devil by trying to live on these trapdoors?

When we think we are safe from moral consequence, O God, arouse us, lest we fall into the chaos of a life undisciplined by thy direction. In Jesus' name. Amen.

Week 49——Day 7   **Read John 8:31**

Edwin Robertson's words are both warning and reminder: "As the Word of God becomes more and more relevant in our everyday life, it will be seen to retain its conditional note, 'This do, and ye shall live.' The understanding of the Word of God is conditional upon obedience. There are no other conditions." There is no way that the truth of the gospel can be

221

understood or demonstrated in some laboratory and then accepted. We can only understand it by obedience. Try it—then you will know it!

God our Father, may we attempt the truth of Christ this day and discover it to be true for us. In Jesus' name. Amen.

WEEK 50

The fruit of the Spirit is . . . patience.—Gal. 5:22

A Candle Called Patience

Week 50——Day 1   Read Ps. 130:5-8

An incident from Lucas Malet's story *The Wages of Sin* has a helpful word that sooner or later we shall all need. The heroine asks her uncle, "What does one do when the sun of one's happiness has set?" He answers, "After a time . . . one lights a candle called patience and guides one's footsteps by that. Try to light your candle of patience, my dear, in faith, remembering that you are not alone. More than half the noblest men and women you meet carry such candles likewise." One cannot command patience merely by willing it. Thank God it is one of the gifts of his Spirit.

O Lord, give us patience to abide the mysteries we cannot understand, to sustain the losses we cannot recover, to endure the disappointments we cannot avoid. In Jesus' name. Amen.

Margaret Fuller once wrote of herself: "I have not yet conquered my own house . . . Shall I raise the siege of this hencoop and march away baffled to a pretended siege of Babylon? It seems to me to do so were to dodge the problem I am set to solve, and to hide my impotency in the thick of the crowd." This is vivid language, but a familiar reflection of ourselves. How busily we rush in self-importance to this crusade or that endeavor or some other engagement—largely because we will not quietly, patiently, devotedly face our own deep needs before God.

Arrest us, our Father, if impatient with the sin within ourselves we go in frantic pursuit of some distant goal and good. Give us patience and courage not to dodge the duty nearest to us. In the name of Christ. Amen.

How exasperating to find a wheat field filled with noxious weeds! The understandable temptation was to rush out and tear up the weeds, but the householder knew this would be poor farming. Jesus tells us it is poor judgment in many life situations. You can't always tell in the early stages which are wheat and which are weeds. Moreover, as Norman Cousins has reminded us, "exasperation is dangerous because it is the natural enemy of responsible judgment. It is the nature of action-born-of-exasperation to produce exactly the opposite effect from the one intended."

Give us wisdom, O God, to know when to wait, and trustful patience in the waiting. In Christ's Spirit. Amen.

Here is a word for someone in a tough or discouraging situation, such as a troublesome church controversy, a frustrating community problem, a trying family difficulty, a broken personal relationship. Are you at the end of your rope, all out of patience, tempted to quit? Paul must have felt this way at Corinth, surrounded by angry disputes, in a soil that promised little for Christian growth. *But he stayed eighteen months!* He was no hit-and-run Christian. Christ never conquers that way. It is only when we stay deeply involved in all the trouble that God can work through us. Christ does not hit and run but waits with us to whatever end may come.

Give us grace, O God, to continue in the struggle for Christ's sake. In his name. Amen.

In Rodgers and Hammerstein's *Carousel* a young man and woman daydream about how wonderful their life together will be. In the lyrics which they sing comes the line, "When today is a long time ago." The words prompt a consideration that ought never to be far from anyone's thought. We cannot know what the outward circumstances of life will be on that distant day; but so far as character and commitment, philosophy and sympathies, are concerned, the future will be a continuation and consequence of the present. What we do while today is today will determine what we will be when today is a long time ago.

Help us, our Father, to lay a good foundation today so that we may take hold of the life which is life indeed. In the Spirit of Christ. Amen.

Eleanor Graham made a sad but sobering observation in her poem "Judgement":

> He died—a hero in the fight—
> And so they crowned his name with light.
> She lived for many a tortured year:
> They only said, "She's getting queer."

Sometimes we fail to recognize some of the true heroes of life—those who carry heavy burdens behind the scenes, those who carefully hide their heartbreak for the sake of others, those who go against custom for the sake of conscience and suffer the ridicule of being called queer.

We would salute all those who have come out of the great tribulation for thee, our Father. In Christ's name. Amen.

In *The New World*, volume two of his *History of the English Speaking Peoples*, Winston Churchill left us this lesson:

In harsh or melancholy epochs free men may always take comfort from the grand lesson of history that tyrannies cannot last except among servile races. The years which seem endless to those who endure them are but a flick of mischance in the journey. New and natural hopes leap from the human heart as every spring revives the cultivated soil and rewards the faithful, patient husbandman.

History's lesson is paralleled by a lesson from our faith that also fosters hope. Patient cultivation of the soil of responding trust and loving witness will give freedom at last from every tyranny.

So may it be. Through Christ our Lord. Amen.

WEEK 51

The fruit of the spirit is . . . goodness.—Gal. 5:22

Give Goodness a Beginning

Week 51——Day 1   Read II Cor. 4:8-10

In his autobiography Albert Schweitzer made this confession:

To the question whether I am a pessimist or an optimist, I answer that my knowledge is pessimistic, but my willing and hoping are optimistic. . . . However much concerned I was at the problem of the misery in the world, I never let myself get lost in broodings over it. I always held firmly to the thought that each one of us can do a little to bring some portion of it to an end.

This, indeed, is all God expects any of us to do—to bring some evil to an end, to give some goodness a beginning. These things we can do with hope and confidence because, with Schweitzer, "we believe in the power of truth and of the Spirit." No Christian can look upon the world today without being cast down, but no Christian can be destroyed, for he knows the power of God to scatter the darkness and redeem the evil.

Give us courage to face the darkness of the times, O God,

and to let thy light shine into darkness, that is around us. For Christ's sake. Amen.

Week 51——Day 2   Read Luke 6:32-36

Jesus' reward for his righteousness was a cross; for his goodness he was crowned with thorns. Lincoln, Gandhi, and Kennedy were assassinated. A great doctor who brought knowledge and comfort in the fight against cancer died herself, a victim of the enemy she fought. Some who live the life of drones die in peace and prosperity at a ripe old age. There is no dependable earthly justice in the way we'd like to figure it.

We remember that whatever the immediate results goodness is better than sin, kindness is better than hardheartedness. Goodness has its reward in the deep inner satisfaction which it brings and in the hope of a closer walk with God. These are gifts of the Spirit.

We would be thy sons, O Most High God. For Jesus' sake. Amen.

Week 51——Day 3   Read Matt. 10:8

James Keller has told us of Eleanor Judd, a blind pianist, who gave her first pint of blood for wounded soldiers back in 1940. As of a few years ago she had given blood seventy-five times, six times the amount of blood in her own body. How many people may owe their lives to her today!

Eleanor Judd's demonstration bears witness to the capacity which God gives to us for his service. In the doing of good we find resources beyond our own endowment. Freely do we

constantly receive (the R.S.V. has it: "received without pay");
freely let us continue to give ("give without pay").

We thank thee, God, for the measure by which thou dost
multiply our strength to do good. For Jesus' sake. Amen.

Week 51——Day 4   Read Exod. 4:1-5

"Nor let my sword sleep in my hand."
Such was William Blake's prayer in a memorable line of
poetry. So does every man need to pray, for swords do sleep
in our hands, even as Moses held a rod of unsuspected and
divine power in his hand. Here is the sword of faith with
which I could do great things, asleep in my hand. Here is the
sword of forgiveness by which I could be reconciled with my
brother, asleep. Here is the sword of mercy by which some
soul in desperate need might be made alive with thanksgiving
and hope, asleep in my hand. Here is the sword of righteousness by which some wrong might be subdued, asleep in my
hand.

Send thy Holy Spirit, O God, that no sword which we could
use for thy victory should lie asleep in our hands. In Christ's
name. Amen.

Week 51——Day 5   Read Luke 8:1-3; 19-25

How did Jesus get through it all? Just to read these verses is
tiring—travels, teaching, healing, a strange and certainly painful
encounter with his misunderstanding family, a dangerous storm
on the lake. We know Jesus drew upon the sustaining resources
of God. And he received them. "Many others . . . provided

for them out of their means." Anonymous people were in the background providing for Jesus and his disciples. It is a high calling, selflessly to serve in order that truth may be known, healing may take place, good work may be done.

O Lord, we thank thee today for all who without recognition or reward serve some purpose in thy kingdom, men and women in homes, schools, offices, hospitals, factories, and churches. In Jesus' name. Amen.

Week 51   Day 6   Read Acts 1:13

One of Kirchoff's famous laws of radiation states: "The absorbing power of substances is proportional to their emitting power." In other words, the best absorbers are the best emitters. The parallel truth in the moral and spiritual realm is not hard to see. Those who absorb most from God are the ones who emit the most for others to receive. Unless, by prayer and by exposure to fine spiritual influences, we absorb a good measure of God, we will have little to emit to others. The reverse is tragically true—let a man carelessly absorb much evil from the world around, and this he will faithfully emit.

God, may it be that people will recognize this day, because of the radiance we emit, that we have been with Jesus. For his sake. Amen.

Week 51——Day 7   Read Matt. 21:28-31

Bernard Shaw's remark gives pause for reflection: "What a man believes may be ascertained not from his creed, but from the assumptions on which he habitually acts."

Sunday: "I believe in the forgiveness of sins."
Monday: "He needn't expect any mercy from me. After all!"
Sunday: "Jesus Christ, the Light of the world."
Monday: "We can't afford to listen to these do-gooders."
Sunday: "He who loses his life for my sake shall find it."
Monday: "Good guys finish last."

We would be willing, our Father, to trust every day the profession we make on any day. Help us. For Jesus' sake. Amen.

WEEK 52

Neither death, nor life, . . . will be able to separate us from the love of God.—Rom. 8:38-39

The Sanctuary of the Ruins

Week 52——Day 1   Read Rom. 8:35-39

The conception and design of the new Coventry Cathedral in England contains much symbolism that points to the great meanings of our faith. The new cathedral has been built at right angles to the old, which was destroyed by bombs in World War II. At the foot of the old tower one looks down what was the nave of the fourteenth century cathedral. Open to the sky it is now the *Sanctuary of the Ruins*. Said Sir Basil Spence, the architect, "The ruins stand clearly for the sacrifice. The new structure stands for the triumph of the resurrection." Even in the ruins of life we find sanctuary when we know

God is there. *In tribulation or distress we are more than conqueror through him who loved us.*

May neither tribulation nor ruin ever destroy our sanctuary in thee, our Father. In Jesus' name. Amen.

Week 52——Day 2　　　　　　　　　**Read Heb. 11:8**

In any venture that moves out beyond the familiar limits of life sooner or later we come to the place where we have to go out "not knowing where we are to go." Every worthwhile undertaking leads us out where our safety is not sure, into ways whose outcome is not known, to do things the world may not approve. This is true of all endeavors for justice, all good works in which we do not seek our own life, in the making of new life after bereavement, punishment, or illness. It is true when we come face to face with death. "Not knowing where . . . ," but in trust of God! If we believe any of these things to be God's call to life, then trust him to go with us and show us the way.

Father, at every turning of the road of life, call me to walk in the way of love, and let me go out in all confidence of thy company. Through Christ our Lord. Amen.

Week 52——Day 3　　　　　　　　　**Read II Cor. 5:6-9**

Cries Cleopatra in Shakespeare's *Anthony and Cleopatra:*

> Give me my robe, put on my crown; I have
> Immortal longings in me.

231

There are among us this very day faithful men and women who speak thus with Cleopatra. They have immortal longings. The time of their departure is close at hand. We pause during this day's meditation to honor our friends and all others for their immortal longings, to pray for them in the time of their going from us, asking that in laying aside all earthly crowns they may inherit a crown of life.

We commend to the safety of thy keeping, O Father, all who come this day into the valley of the shadow of death. For Christ's sake. Amen.

Week 52——Day 4   Read Luke 24:5

Mary and the other women who came to Joseph's garden made the same mistake we all make—seeking the living among the dead. Jesus was not in the tomb. We will not find those we love in the grave, but alive in our hearts. They are clothed with a body of the spirit. They dwell in eternity, and we must look for them among the living. Personal effects, grave markers, pictures—these help us remember. But never, never must we think that a living soul in love with God is imprisoned anywhere with the dead. They are alive. They are everywhere we are, free in the glorious liberty of the children of God in the communion of saints.

We thank thee, our Father, that we do not ever have to visit our dead in the prison house of death. For they are set free to be alive with thee. Through Jesus Christ our Lord. Amen.

> Say to those who are of a fearful heart,
> "Be strong, fear not!
> Behold, your God
>   will come . . .
>   . . . and save you."

These words are part of the Christian commital service. But how could we have the boldness to read that at the moment of unutterable anguish beside an open grave? Boldness it is, but not mockery. Because the promise is from God, who has shown us the strength of his mighty arm and who in Christ demonstrated his power over death. The wonderful vision and images of Isaiah's faith are both sweet consolation and mighty incentive to the faithful living of our days.

In the glorious confidence of our everlasting hope let us return to the duties of our days with devotion and joy, O God. In Christ's name. Amen.

A popular song has it, "I'll see you again, whenever spring breaks through again." Such could be the Christian song in the face of death. A great spirit once said to his family just before he died, "I'll be seeing you!" Jesus said the same words to his disciples in the upper room, "You will see me." God is love, and we live in each other's love with him. This wonderful knowledge can turn the sadness of death to the joy of reunion. On some day, far off in time here, but only a moment there, a knock will come upon a "door," a voice will "speak" our name. Then a face will appear, a soul loved long since but lost only for a while.

Confirm the promise of our faith, O eternal Spirit. Through our risen Lord. Amen.

Week 52——Day 7   **Read Luke 24:1-11**

The resurrection is no *idle tale*. It seemed such to the apostles when they first heard it. They could not believe what the women told them—until they met the risen Lord for themselves. The resurrection always seems an idle tale when someone else merely tells us about it. But then we meet the living Christ. We meet him in the assurance of God's forgiveness. We meet him in the reconciling ministry of his Church in lives which have been transformed by the risen Christ. We meet him in the joy which comes as we begin by trustful obedience to do the things he has commanded. No longer does it seem an idle tale. We know it is true because we know *him*—not a theory, but a person.

Even so, come, Lord Jesus, that we may believe. Amen.

WEEK 53

Choose this day whom you will serve.—Josh. 24:15

The Moment of Truth

Week 53——Day 1   **Read I Sam. 17:31-37**

One ought really to read this entire chapter; it is one of the great stories of scripture. But these seven verses are central for they depict a man in his *moment of truth*. Irving Stone describes in *The Agony and the Ecstasy* how Michelangelo wrestled within himself to know how to depict David in his massive statue. He decided to show David in the moment of his decision to fight rather than in the later moment of victory. Why? Because the thing that made David great was his decision that Israel must be free from vassalage, not his killing of Goliath. Decision is more important than execution. Character is more critical than results.

Our Father, stand beside us in every moment of truth in which we must decide whom we will serve. Neither for fear nor favor may we refuse to decide for goodness, freedom, and truth in the choices of this day, and always. In the Spirit of Christ. Amen.